Twelve Steps to a New Day

For Teens

Ron Keller

A JANET THOMA BOOK

Thomas Nelson Publishers
Nashville

The accounts of individuals's lives presented in this book are fictitious and are composites based on the author's clinical experience with hundreds of people through the years. Any resemblance between the characters in the stories and actual persons is coincidental.

Published in Nashville, Tennessee, by Thomas Nelson, Inc., and distributed in Canada by Lawson Falle, Ltd., Cambridge, Ontario.

All direct Scripture quotations are from the NEW KING JAMES VERSION of the Bible. Copyright © 1979, 1980, 1982, Thomas Nelson, Inc., Publishers.

Other references to the Scriptures are paraphrases of passages from:
J. B. Phillips: THE NEW TESTAMENT IN MODERN ENGLISH, Revised Edition. Copyright © J. B. Phillips 1958, 1960, 1972. Used by permission of Macmillan Publishing Co., Inc.
THE JERUSALEM BIBLE. Copyright © 1966 by Darton, Longman & Todd, Ltd. and Doubleday & Company, Inc. Used by permission.
The Holy Bible: NEW INTERNATIONAL VERSION are marked NIV. Copyright © 1978 by the New York International Bible Society. Used by permission of Zondervan Bible Publishers.
TODAY'S ENGLISH VERSION: *The Good News Bible*, Old Testament © 1976 by the American Bible Society; New Testament © 1966, 1971, 1976 American Bible Society. Used by permission.

Library of Congress Cataloging-in-Publication Data

Keller, Ron.
    The twelve steps to a new day for teens / by Ron Keller.
        p.   cm.
    ISBN 0-8407-7797-3
    1. Church group work with teenagers.   2. Twelve-step programs—
Religious aspects—Christianity.   3. Teenagers—Religious life.
I. Title. II. Title: 12 steps to a new day for teens.
BV4447.K454   1993
248.8′3—dc20
                                        92-21046
                                           CIP

Printed in the United States of America
1 2 3 4 5 6 - 97 96 95 94 93

To
_____

My father, P. J. Keller,
who died on September 22, 1988.
As this work was coming into full life,
his earthly life at age sixty-three was coming to an end.

Contents

Acknowledgments

Nancy, my understanding wife, who has been faithful and supportive.

Janet Thoma for her clear editorial guidance.

Gail Steel, president of Prince of Peace Publishing, Inc., Burnsville, Minnesota, for her unselfish commitment and dedication to the success of this project.

DeWayne Herbrandson, for his commitment to making this book happen by serving as consultant and agent.

Mary Wagnild, for her word processing and editing.

Our children, Matthew, Brigitte, Peter, Joshua, and Jonathan, for their quiet support and encouragement.

A very special thanks to Brigitte, Peter, Steve, Molly, Dave, Melissa, Amy, Natie, Julie, Steve, Tony, Eileen, Tammy, Carol, Jill, Catherine, John, Daniel, Bob, Matt, Rich, and Mark Conway.

The Twelve Steps for Teenagers

Step 1: I admit that I am powerless over certain parts of my life and I need God's help.

We were powerless, when at just the right time Christ died for us. (Rom. 5:6).

Step 2: I am coming to believe that Jesus Christ came in a human body, that He is here with me now in Spirit, and that He has the power to change my weaknesses into strengths.

Jesus Christ is the visible expression of the invisible God. All things were created by Him and for Him, and He holds all things in unity (Col. 1:15–17).

Step 3: I turn my will and my life over to Jesus Christ, my Lord and Savior.

I have been crucified with Christ. It is no longer I who live, but Christ who lives in me. And the life I now live in the flesh, I live by faith in the Son of Man who loved me and gave His life for me (Gal. 2:20).

Step 4: I begin honestly listing what I know and discover about myself: my strengths, weaknesses, and behavior.

I am wonderful, and my soul knows this very well. Lord, examine me and know my heart. Probe me and know my thoughts. Make sure I do not follow harmful ways (Ps. 139:14, 23).

Step 5: I am ready to honestly share with God and another person the exact nature of my strengths, weaknesses, and behavior.

Confess your sins to one another, and pray for one another. In this way you will be healed (James 5:16).

Step 6: I am entirely ready to have Jesus Christ heal all those areas of my life that need His touch.

All those who touched Jesus were healed (Mark 6:56b).

The Twelve Steps for Teenagers

▼

Step 7: I humbly ask Jesus Christ to change my weaknesses into strengths so that I will become more like Him.

If we acknowledge our sin, He is faithful and just. He will forgive us and purify us from everything that is wrong (1 John 1:9).

Step 8: I make a list of the people I have hurt and become willing to go to them to mend the relationship.

By the love that you have for one another, the world will know that you are My disciples (John 13:34–35).

Step 9: I make amends with the people I have hurt, except when to do so might bring harm to them or others.

If you remember that your brother or sister has something against you, leave your offering there before the altar, go and be reconciled to your brother or sister first, and then come back and present your offering (Matt 5:23–24).

Step 10: Each day I do a review of myself and my activities. When I am wrong, I quickly admit it. When I am right, I thank God for the guidance.

Let each examine his own conduct (Gal. 6:4).

Step 11: To keep growing in my relationship with Jesus Christ, I spend time each day praying and reading the Bible. I will gather with others who do the same. I ask Jesus for guidance and the power to do what He wants me to do.

Remain in Me. If you remain in Me and My words abide in you, you may ask what you will, and you will get it (John 15:7).

Step 12: I am grateful that God is changing me through these Twelve Steps. In response, I will reach out to share Christ's love by practicing these principles in all that I do.

Whatever you did to the least of My brothers, you did it to Me (Matt 25:40).

The Twelve Steps for Teenagers: A Revolutionary Life-Style

THE PROBLEM

"Every kid in America must have problems like I do. I can't possibly be the only one who is having such a hard time with life," Sharon shared with us in a small group meeting at a friend's house. Sharon came from an alcoholic family. Her father was unpredictable. It was scary for Sharon to live in her house. And she admitted she felt all alone.

"Can you guys tell me a little bit about what life is like for you?" she asked. "Or am I the only who feels like I'm going crazy?"

"I don't think I have problems as big as yours," Todd said, "but I know I am always having some kind of trouble. I used to blame my parents because they're never home. But lately I've been looking at my own stuff—not just theirs. I have to learn to make a life for myself," he said. "A decent life, not just this partying stuff. I'm tired of the way I live."

Although the group had been meeting for years, this particular grouping of kids was meeting for the first time. At every meeting new kids would come, and some of the regulars wouldn't be there.

Many of the eleven kids gathered had known one another a long time. Some had been a part of the group for as long as three years. One was Jenny.

"I hate to admit it to you guys," Jenny said, "but I am constantly comparing myself with other people. I even do it with you. I feel so inferior. I wake up in the morning, and the first thing I think about is how worthless I am in comparison to everyone else in the world."

Everyone was silent. Jenny's honesty was helping the kids in the group get in touch with how they felt about themselves. The adult leader of the group reached out and put her hand on Jenny's shoulder. She didn't say anything. She didn't need to. Everyone knew that she cared about the kids in that room.

"I don't know about you," Sharon jumped in, "but I think a lot of my bad feelings about myself come from my family situation. I hate living at home. I'm embarrassed about my dad's drinking. I never know what he'll do next. I can never have any of my friends over."

"I gotta tell you," Steve said, "life has been good for me lately, and I have you all to thank. I remember coming here seven weeks ago and complaining about my parents and how old-fashioned they are. Do you remember the night? I wanted to run away. And you guys helped me see how stupid that would be."

Steve, a well-dressed, popular, funny junior in high school, went on. "I did the Ninth Step just like you told me to. As hard as it was for me, I went to Mom and apologized for yelling at her like I did, and everything has changed since then. Thanks."

All the kids in the room respected Steve. They appreciated the good things he had just shared. They felt the good feelings with him. After a few moments of silence, Jan, the leader, noticed that John had tears in his eyes. "Is there something you'd like to say, John?" she asked. John stuttered for words.

"I don't know if I'll ever get over Ken (his friend who had been killed in a car accident three months previous to the meeting). I miss him so much, and I still feel so guilty that I didn't do more for him. I just want to give up and die."

All the kids in the group felt bad for John. They, too, missed Ken. His death was a tragedy to most kids at the school. Late on a Friday night, after he had been drinking, he ran into a bridge. His death was sudden and shocking.

The kids listened carefully to John. Their silence was an indication of their respect and love for him. Their hearts went out to him as they assured him of their prayer and love.

That meeting was held more than thirty years ago. It was a meeting of Alateen, a gathering for the sons and daughters of alcoholic parents. I was there, I saw all that happen. I experienced it for myself. My dad was an alcoholic.

That meeting—and now many others like it—are reminders that every kid has problems to deal with. No kid gets through life without difficulties...some more trying than others. We found that we could help one another by sharing parts of our lives. We learned how to do that in high school, and we now do it as adults.

Using the Twelve Steps and passages from the Bible, we have found a way to live rich, full lives, regardless of our problems.

GROWING UP IS COMPLICATED

Growing up is tough. Scary. Lonely. Frustrating.

Growing up is complicated and confusing. There are so many decisions to make. And most of them demand choices before kids are ready to make them. Most of the important decisions I had to make as a teenager seemed to come before I was equipped to make them, decisions like the ones expressed by these teens:

- "It's hard to be a teenager because there are so many pressures put on you to be the 'perfect' person in everyone's eyes. You have to have a good head on your shoulders and be happy with yourself. You have to make your own decisions and be careful about the friends you choose." *Julie*
- "I am scared and worried. Will there be nuclear war? What is happening to the environment? Will there still be starvation and hardships? What about drug abuse and teenage pregnancy?" *Laura*
- "I am afraid of totally bumming out on life, becoming an addict and making nothing of the life God gave me. I want to live my life to help people and learn about life." *Natie*
- "I am afraid of how selfish I am. All I think about is me and my life. I really don't care about anyone or anything else." *Roger*

Growing up is challenging. We have to think carefully about what we should do and whom we should spend time with. These mental struggles get even more complicated by the bodily changes that we experience. And all that gets even more difficult when we add the constant invitations to have sex, watch more videos, do drugs and liquor, and listen to more and more heavy metal music. These and other suggestions come from our peers and within ourselves.

"Whom should I listen to? How should I act? What should I do and not do? How should I live my life?" These questions can get even more complicated if we don't have a good relationship with our parents, or if our parents are divorced or busy or away from home.

Think about your own life. What are your particular problems?

HOW ABOUT YOU?

Please take a few minutes to answer the questions below. Throughout the book, you'll read answers from other teens.

My biggest problem right now is (for example, I don't have one really good friend)

dealing w/ Cole; a non-bf hu I've mixed feelings about & overall struggling w/ guys & my "flirting."

If I could change one thing in my life right now, it would be (for example, my family situation; I know it's lousy, but I can't seem to change it)

my "happiness" when I meet people esp. guys.

The biggest mistake I've ever made is (for instance, stealing my neighbor's car)

going crazy & acting really hyper/ blowing up @ my rents

When I think of my future, I feel (for instance, excited; I'm looking forward to twelfth grade)

nervous, unsure; I'm scared about high school & all its craps & stuff.

Why? (For instance, I'm looking forward to being on my own and away from home)

I'm afraid of the material & worldly demand & pressures ex: music, moovies, clothes, long.

I get most excited right now about *(for instance, going to the concert on Saturday night)*

having an opportunity to talk with some friends & fellowship on Friday (mayb school?)

Here are a few answers other teens mentioned when they thought about their biggest problems. You might check the ones that also apply to you.

✓ "My biggest problem right now is trying to find myself and please others at the same time." *Jill*

___ "My biggest problem right now is lack of confidence in myself. Sometimes I depend too heavily on other people to tell me who I am." *Jessica*

✓ "My biggest problem right now is getting people to like me." *Bill*

___ "My biggest problem right now is that I'm in a fight with one of my best friends." *Julie*

✓ "My biggest problem right now is establishing myself in a new school." *Matt*

✓ "My biggest problem right now is learning how to feel good about the way I am. I'm way too self-conscious." *Beth*

✓ "My problem is getting my schedule to work out. I'm always very busy, and I need to find some time when I can just relax and not worry about all my obligations." *Art*

___ "My biggest problem right now is my family life. It seems that we're always fighting. Every time I turn around they're telling me that I'm a brat or that I'm selfish, or they're telling me what to do. I'm also having problems with my friends. I seem to get sick of them." *Ellen*

___ "My biggest problem right now is justifying my existence and trying to find my true purpose in life." *Brett*

THE TWELVE STEPS FOR TEENAGERS

Growing up in an alcoholic family and working with kids since I have been an adult, I have made four important discoveries. These discoveries have helped me find a way to bring the Twelve Steps into everyday life.

1. We all have problems that we live with every day. Some problems are here today and gone tomorrow, like getting a bad grade, having a fight with a best friend, losing a toothbrush, or missing a party. This kind of problem goes away.

2. We all have problems that don't go away. They stay with us. They hurt. These are problems like death, divorce, fear, loneliness, school problems, personality problems, brother/sister problems, Mom/Dad problems. These problems hang around and never seem to go away. What do we do about them? How do we handle them?

3. There's a way to live with these "permanent" problems. We can learn a way of life that makes life good even when life's bad.

4. No matter how hard life is, Jesus Christ has promised that He has come to bring us a full life. You can have that life. The Twelve Steps help teens live fuller, richer lives in all kinds of circumstances.

HOW THE TWELVE STEPS FOR TEENAGERS CAN HELP YOU

The original Twelve Steps as well as many other Twelve-Step programs have been used for years and have helped millions of people. The Twelve Steps address all of life's major problems, issues, and struggles.

The original Twelve-Step program was and is still used by alcoholics. The Steps have been a simple, straightforward way for them to get the help they need to stop drinking. The Steps also help them to change those parts of their lives that made their disease worse.

For about thirty years, many other people have benefited from Twelve-Step programs by applying the Steps to their specific problems and needs. In groups like Alateen, the Steps have helped kids with alcoholic parents to cope with the horrible struggles that often take place in that type of family. Other groups like Narc-Anon, Al-Anon, Overeaters Anonymous, and Emotions Anonymous, to name a few, have also used Twelve-Step programs to improve the lives of their members.

The Twelve Steps for Teenagers are designed for all kids who need help with daily living. All honest kids know they can use all the help they can get just to make it in life. Besides the issues of daily life, every teenager has an unusual problem or struggle that makes life even more difficult. The Twelve Steps for Teenagers are helpful to kids any time but especially when hard times come along.

I kind of grew up with the Twelve Steps. Through them, my family, and my friends, I learned how to live with problems and still have a good life.

After I got out of college, I met the greatest person who has ever walked on this earth. His name is Jesus Christ. Ever since I opened my life to Him, He has given me the privilege of working for Him and with Him. It has been the most exciting thing that could ever happen to anyone.

My life is dedicated to Him because of what He did for me. He loves me no matter what I do or have done. The first time that sank into my brain, I was overwhelmed.

Because He has done so much for me, I wanted to bring Him into everything I do. (I know He's there already, but I wanted more people to know that He's there.)

So, a few years ago, I took those same Twelve Steps that have been used by people with a drinking problem, and I rearranged them a little bit. I put the name of Jesus right smack in the center of the Steps because I believe there is no greater name in all of history. And I included Bible verses to support each Step. Those Steps, as I have revised them, appear on pages viii–ix. I hope you'll read them, talk about them, make them your own and, most of all, do them.

DO YOU NEED THE TWELVE STEPS FOR TEENAGERS?

These Twelve Steps have been written for every teenager. But before they'll work for you, you'll need to be convinced that you need them.

Check the items that are true for you.

_____ Do you feel that you've never had a break in life?
_____ Do you cover up your real feelings? Do you often pretend?
_____ Do you have many unanswered questions about God? About death?

✓ Do you sometimes do or say strange or shocking things just to get attention?

___ Do you feel unloved, uncared for?

___ Do you worry about your parents, brothers, and/or sisters?

✓ Do you feel afraid?

___ Do you avoid going home because you dislike it there?

___ Do you consider running away from your problems by using drugs, alcohol, or other chemicals or by listening to TV or audio tapes or CD's?

___ Do you go to extremes to get people to like you?

___ Is it difficult for you to talk with your parents about important things?

✓ Do you feel lonely?

✓ Do you have trouble concentrating on your schoolwork?

✓ Do you lose your temper often?

✓ Do you have some things in your life that you'd like to change and have wanted to change for a long time?

___ Are there things in your life that you've tried to change but couldn't?

✓ Are you frustrated?

✓ Is it hard for you to be honest and share your true feelings with your friends?

✓ Do you have a poor relationship with God?

The Twelve-Step process addresses all of the major problems kids deal with. This book helps you identify the problems in your life. It helps you think clearly about those problems. It provides a place for you to talk about them when you feel ready.

If you are looking for help, you've found it. Your relationship with yourself, God, and others will get better using this straightforward approach.

How to Use This Book

This book was created for you to use as a tool to discover more about yourself. Write in it. Mark it up!

This is a workbook—your workbook—but not like any other you've ever used. You write your own story in this book. For many kids, this book has become their best friend. As they write in it a little bit at a time, from month to month and year to year, they see changes that have taken place in their lives. It becomes their life story in writing.

You don't need to rush through this book. It is a fun process to be involved in. It is not a program. It is not a textbook you'll be tested on. Many kids have gone through these Twelve Steps many times, over and over again. Go slowly. Let them help you address some of your bad feelings and experiences in life.

This book has been designed so that you can use it many times as well. On one step, you may answer only one question and then move on to the next step. It's okay to leave some unfinished parts. Use the book long enough to get you thinking, feeling, and sharing. The goal is to use the book as a tool to discover and experience a richer, better life.

When you go through the book the second, third, or fourth time, you will be surprised as you compare your answers now to what they were then.

Each chapter deals with one of the Twelve Steps. Each chapter usually begins with one or several short true stories. At the end of the stories you are sometimes asked to write your own answers to directed questions in the section "How About You?"

That is usually followed by the section "What the Bible Says About

Step _____." Rather than rush through all the passages, you might like to use one passage a day.

The last section of each chapter is "My Reflections on Step _____." You apply the principles of each chapter to your life situation by writing a few words that describe what you've learned or how you feel.

I suggest you try to work on one step each week. After you've gone through Step Twelve, go back to Step One and begin the process at a deeper level. Each time you go through the Steps, focus on a word, phrase, or theme that helps you through the day and week. The significant thing is not how much of this book you get done; it's how well you apply these ideas that bring changes to your life. Following this suggested format, you would go through the Steps about four times per year (forty-eight weeks).

The Steps do not necessarily follow each other. If possible, it is best to work one step after another, but no one thoroughly completes one step before moving to another. You can jump in at any step and still benefit from the process. You do not have to begin with Step One. You can benefit from the principles in Step Four, even if you aren't familiar with Step One. It is usually best, however, to move through the Twelve Steps in twelve weeks and then return again to Step One.

Most people who leave a step to move on to the next step leave it with an unfinished feeling. That's okay because this is a process...a lifelong process. Discovering yourself and getting closer to other people and God are the ultimate goals of this book. Let God help you, lead you, and guide you.

You will find that the first four steps are the longest and most likely the most challenging. Please do not get discouraged. By doing a little bit at a time, you will sense progress.

So, here's what I suggest you do.

Read one step each day of an entire week. Spend six minutes first thing in the morning and six minutes last thing at night to read or memorize the reading that follows each step.

Write. Put your thoughts down in the spaces provided. Check off your answers to the questions for each step. Write or draw in the white spaces. Circle words. Underline phrases.

Go easy. When you go through the Steps, do what you can on each one. Some other time, when you go through the Steps again, you can work on whatever else needs to be done. Don't rush.

Group Covenant

The name of our group is ——————————————— Twelve Steps for Teenagers.

We will meet at *(beginning time)*———— until *(closing time)*———— each *(day)*———— beginning on *(date)*————.

We will meet at least twelve weeks. After the twelve weeks, we promise to be honest in evaluating this group. We might continue the group if we so agree.

We promise to be honest.
We will do our best to come prepared.
We promise to help one another.
We will pray for one another.
We will listen to one another without interrupting.

For this twelve-week period, we choose ——— to ——— not to have others join us.

Date: ————————————   Signature: ————————————————

Group leader: ————————————————   Phone:————————

Others Attending   Phone

—————————————————————   ————————————
—————————————————————   ————————————
—————————————————————   ————————————
—————————————————————   ————————————
—————————————————————   ————————————
—————————————————————   ————————————
—————————————————————   ————————————
—————————————————————   ————————————
—————————————————————   ————————————
—————————————————————   ————————————

HOW TO DO THE TWELVE STEPS FOR TEENAGERS

There are three ways to do the Twelve Steps for Teenagers: (1) alone, (2) in a group, or (3) alone and in a group.

It's true that you'll benefit a great deal by doing the Steps alone. However, you'll get the most support and growth by being involved in a group at the same time that you do the Steps yourself.

On page 11, you'll find a group covenant and a sample sheet for the names and phone numbers of group members. If no group meets in your area, give this book to an adult friend. Ask that person to help you get a group started. Maybe you're in an existing group that could use these Steps. Suggest that to your group leader.

WALKING THROUGH THE TWELVE STEPS FOR TEENAGERS IS AN ADVENTURE

The Steps will call you into honesty like you have never experienced before. You will discover yourself. Taking risks and being honest will be very challenging sometimes. Being honest may cause you some pain for a while. But the freedom you find will make the risks and the pain very worthwhile.

This adventure, the Twelve Steps for Teenagers, is an adventure with yourself. You can work on only one person—you. The Twelve Steps are an adventure with God. You can learn more about His love for you. And the Twelve Steps are an adventure with others.

It's a growing process. It's a great idea. It's fun. And you will be set free!

CHAPTER 1

I Feel Hopeless

Step One:

I admit that I am powerless over certain parts of my life and I need God's help.

FEELING HOPELESS

When I was a teenager living with my family, the biggest problem I had to live with every day was my dad's drinking. He was an alcoholic. I never knew what to expect. Would he be drunk or sober? Did he mean what he was saying, or didn't he? Could I count on him or not? Would he embarrass me? His alcoholism affected me in many ways. I was scared about him and his disease. I missed having a father. I was lonely.

When I was fifteen years old, I realized there was nothing I could do about the situation. I couldn't change my dad or anyone else. I could only change myself and the way I looked at things. That first step helped me. It helped me to admit that I was powerless over the circumstances. I had no power to change my dad or myself. I admitted my need for God's help. Fortunately, for the last five years of his life, my dad and I had a great relationship. I discovered many of his good qualities that I hadn't previously recognized. Our relationship had an unusually happy ending.

I am still learning to live with the fact that I will always be powerless over certain parts of my life. Being powerless means I am without power, force, or energy. It means I am weak; I am not able to produce any effect or change. I am powerless over some of my own personality defects. I'm judgmental. I'm a perfectionist. I'm an idealaholic (I think everything should be ideal). I'm a workaholic.

I still admit, daily, my need for God's help. I need His help, today more than ever, in little and big things. And I will always need His help.

Every kid has problems to deal with. "You're always feeling bad about your own situation until you run into somebody who's really got it bad. Like, I always felt bad that I couldn't get on the basketball team until I met this one kid who doesn't even have legs. That's bad," Tony told me one day after a teen group meeting.

Every teenager needs to learn how to live in a healthy way. We may be born with the ability to live a healthy life, but our culture messes us up and we have to learn how to live all over again.

It is very important to know ourselves, our problems, and our addictions. It is important to know what we are powerless over and what we must accept because we cannot change that thing or problem.

It is just as important to admit our problems and addictions to ourselves and to God. By denying these parts of ourselves, we deny who we are. When we admit the truth—our powerlessness to change some things—we find freedom, hope, and the strength to cope with things the way they are.

Kids have noteworthy things to say about these areas.

- John is upset because his parents don't spend any time with him.
- Carol is disappointed because neither one of her parents ever comes to her activities. They always talk about it but never show up.
- Tom is always worried about his mom and dad. He's afraid that someday soon he's going to walk into the house and one of them will be gone.
- Ted is afraid of his fierce anger. He has tried to figure out where it comes from. He is afraid that he is going to hurt someone someday. He says he needs help in getting it worked out.

Lots of kids feel helpless and hopeless. They want to give up. They don't know what to do. They are convinced that life will always be this way for them. It could. Unless they do something about it. The place to begin is admitting that they need help from God and other people.

TAKING STEP ONE

Terry was a reserved kid. He seldom talked to anyone. He was good at football, and from what kids knew of him, he seemed to be a nice guy. His parents and other adults were concerned about him. They weren't worried because he was into bad stuff; they were concerned because he never really expressed himself.

Like his father, Terry kept everything to himself. He didn't see a need for talking with others. In fact, it seemed that he didn't need anybody else for anything.

The truth is, Terry had problems, like we all do. He kept them inside. He didn't admit to his powerlessness over his problems. He didn't admit his need for other people to be a part of his life and his need for God (at least openly).

His life ended when he kept his car running and closed the garage doors. Apparently, he had been suffering silently for years. He chose to keep his problems inside. The problems ate away at him until finally he could not deal with them anymore.

Knowing your problems is very important. Admitting them to yourself and others is very healthy. But where do you go for help with these things? Or do you have to live like this for the rest of your life?

Many adults are willing to help. They can give encouragement and guidance. Most likely your parents are the two most important adults in your life who are eager to do that for you.

But more than that, God is with you. He knows you. He wants to help. And He will help you. He helps those who are powerless, the lost, the sinners, and the sick.

Why God? What does God have to do with these Steps?

HOW ABOUT YOU?

What is your impression of God right now? (Check ones that seem most appropriate for you.)

kinda all

____ God is like a parent.
____ God is like a police officer.
____ God is almighty, able to do everything.
____ I have my own impression of God that I can't describe.
____ The best impression I have of God is in Jesus Christ.
____ God is a distant Spirit.

Your god is what you think about most. Who or what is your god right now?

School, cole?, God

The more you can identify what your problems are, the sooner you can get help and become a healthier person. From the following suggestions, choose those that seem to be your areas of struggle right now.

My struggles (check the things listed that have become so important to you that they are gods in your life, addictions):

____ TV   ____ Drugs
____ Phone   ____ Movies/VCR
____ Feeling guilty   ____ Music
____ Laziness   ____ Excitement
____ Sex   ____ Stress
____ Alcohol   _X_ Homework
____ Chocolate   _?_ A relationship
____ Food   ____ Soft drinks
____ Sports   _X_ Being "cool"
____ _____   ____ Myself

My main problem today:

____ My body (I don't like it.)
____ Mom
____ Dad
____ What I think about my mom or dad
____ My brother
____ My sister
____ My face
____ My friend
_?_ Boyfriend/girlfriend
____ Money
_X_ School
     _X_ Grades
     ____ A teacher
____ Job
_X_ Future
____ Too many secrets that I need to keep
____ My past
____ Others:
     _X_ *Managing my time – social + academic*
____ _____

___ _____

___ _____

___ _____

God and His Son, Jesus, promised to help us with our problems. Read these promises each day this week:

> I, Jesus, am telling you not to worry about your life and what you are to eat, nor about your body and what kind of clothes you are to wear. Surely life means more than food, and the body more than clothing! Look at the birds in the sky. They don't sow or reap or gather into barns; yet the Lord feeds them. Are you not worth much more than they are? Can any of you, for all your worrying, add one single minute to your life span? And why worry about clothing? Think of the flowers growing in the fields; they never have to work or spin; yet I assure you that not even Solomon in all his royal garb was robed like one of these. Now if that is how God clothes the grass in the field, which is there today and thrown into the furnace tomorrow, will the Lord not much more look after you, you of little faith? So do not worry; do not say, "What are we to eat? What are we to drink? How are we to be clothed?" It is the pagans who set their hearts on all these things. Your heavenly Master knows you need them all. Set your hearts first on the Lord's kingdom and righteousness, and all these other things will be given you as well. So, don't worry about tomorrow: tomorrow will take care of itself. Each day has enough trouble of its own (Matt. 6:25–34).

Jesus has helped me all my life. I know thousands of other people in the world that He has helped. God can help you with all problems—big and small. He created the world we live in. He made you and me. He knows what He is doing (in fact, He is really the only one who knows what He is doing).

He can help you. He will help you. Think about your life.

1. Which situations cause the most worry for you? (Choose one or several.)

_____ Zits   _____ Being grounded
_____ Arguments with Mom/Dad   _____ Having a date
_____ Gossiping friends   _1_X_ Schoolwork/grades
_2_X_ Being alone   _____ My car
_____ My mouth   _3_?X_ $$$
_3_X_ _guy relat._   _____ _____

2. What do you think is the worst thing that could happen in this situation? (*For instance, Mom and Dad could get divorced. I could get hurt in football.*)

I make a major fool out of myself & shun away my friends & then start failing my classes.

3. What is the best thing that could happen in this situation? (*For instance, Mom and Dad will come back together in a new way. I could get a year off football practice to study more and improve my grades.*)

I'll make tons of new friends Azian & non-Azian, my friends'll ♥ me & put ↑ w/ me & I'll do gr8 & get good grades all yr. ←(?)

4. What can you do to stop worrying? (*For instance, talk to my parents and let them know I am worried about them. Pray. Read the Bible more.*)

Know that my friends like me 4 hu I am. Pray & ask G 4 encouragement & help.

5. Describe a situation in your past where you felt powerless (you had no power to change the situation):

my grandfather passing away w/o knowing F

What did it feel like? *(For instance, I was always the shortest and youngest one in my class. Kids made fun of me. I felt humiliated.)*

I felt guilty 4 not reaching out 2 him & ping him the way I should have

What did you do about it? *(For example, I was angry and sometimes yelled at other kids when they talked about how little I was.)*

cried & talked 2 my mom a little + prayed 2 god

6. In what area of your life do you feel powerless now? How are you handling it? *(For example, I do not have a good relationship with my dad. He is gone almost all the time. I handle it by pretending that I don't care.)*

reaching Cole & telling him about G & helping him get over his prob. & bad stuff.

7. Have you ever asked for God's help? ✓ yes ____ no
What happened? *(For instance, when I was in fifth grade, I asked God to help my parents stop fighting. He answered my prayer.)*

w somethin out w track, gennom, & cheerleading & he did.

8. What is Jesus telling you to do in the reading on page 19? What is worth worrying about? *(For example, Jesus is telling me not to worry about my dad. He has his life, and I have mine. He will be home more and spend time with me when he wants to. I can't control that.)*

G's plan is perfect & just keep trying & t let G's plan itt wk out

_____

_____

Now let's look at a few passages in the Bible written by people like you and me who needed God's help.

WHAT THE BIBLE SAYS ABOUT STEP ONE

I admit that I am powerless over certain parts of my life and I need God's help.

Choose one passage from the selections given and read it each day during the next week. Think about the passage by checking the statements that describe how you feel. Then write a few words about how this passage applies to you.

1. A great leader in the early church, Paul, wrote these encouraging words to his friends while he was suffering in prison:

There is nothing I cannot master with the help of Jesus, the one who gives me strength (Phil. 4:13).

____ I have problems that seem to be major.
____ I can handle them because Jesus is with me and gives me strength.
____ I don't feel like I have any problems in my life right now.
✔ _I have minor prob. + my life's purty good, but I'm conscience about my grades + witnessing 2 friends_

2. King David wrote these important and familiar words as a song of trust. He believed that God was his personal shepherd:

Because the Lord is my shepherd, I have everything I need (Ps. 23:1).

____ I don't need a shepherd. I have everything I need.

___ What more could I want than to have the Lord as my guide and leader?
___ Because He is that for me, I have everything I need.

___ _____
_____
_____

MY REFLECTIONS ON STEP ONE

I admit that I am powerless over certain parts of my life and I need God's help.

What do you think about Step One? Write down your feelings, thoughts, and ideas.

_____
_____
_____
_____
_____
_____
_____
_____
_____

Exercise: This week, be brave enough to admit some area of powerlessness. Ask for God's help. Let go. Turn your worries over to Him.

For further study:

• Romans 7:15–25
• John 8:34–36
• Romans 8:1–3
• 1 Corinthians 10:12–14

CHAPTER 2

One Who Is Greater Than I Brings Hope

Step Two:

*I am coming to believe that
Jesus Christ came in a human body, that
He is here with me now in Spirit, and
that He has the power to change
my weaknesses into strengths.*

ONE WHO IS GREATER THAN I BRINGS HOPE

Jan knew that she had a problem with food. Most of the time she ate when she wasn't even hungry. She stuffed herself with snacks and then hated herself for it.

Because she was afraid of gaining weight, she threw up. It was a pattern that had been going on a long time in her life, so long, Jan almost accepted it as normal. As time went on, however, she lost too much weight and looked anemic. Her family and friends were very concerned about her.

She wanted to stop the pattern. She tried for months. She knew she couldn't do it by herself. On her own she didn't have the power or ability to make the change. Mostly, she didn't know why she was doing it.

Finally, Jan became ashamed and felt guilty about her behavior and decided to ask for help. She found that she and many other girls in her school had a problem called bulimia. Together, with her family, Jan rediscovered what it means to have real life, to be a Christian, and to ask Jesus to help deal with her weaknesses.

Jan accepted Jesus' love for her. Unworthy as she felt, she received His forgiveness. She experienced Jesus in a different way. Knowing that she was powerless, she felt safe in reaching out to Him. He was there for her.

As a teenager, you are in the process of growing up. You are becoming what you will be. You are not completely there yet. You have lived less than one-fourth your life. You are on the way toward something. That is a tough spot to be in. Thankfully, it is short and temporary.

You feel that something more for you is out there, something beyond where you are now. You are in process. You are in between adolescence and adulthood. Being in between can be very frustrating. You are neither a kid nor an adult. For a little while longer it will be this way. Everyone goes through this phase in life. You are going through physical, emotional, social, and spiritual changes, all at the same time. Adults go through some of the same changes but in different ways and not all four areas at one time.

You are obviously going to make mistakes and have areas of weakness when you are growing. Taking Step Two can help you deal with your weaknesses and move on, just as Joan did.

TAKING STEP TWO

Joan was born with legs that didn't function. She was disabled from the beginning of her life. She was in hospitals and other institutions most of the time. Her health worsened as time went on. One physical problem led to another. Eventually, one of her legs had to be amputated. The surgery and the aftermath caused many complications.

Joan spent day after day lying in bed and asking, "God, why is it like this? Why can't I be like other kids? Why don't You heal me? How can I ever be useful to anyone this way?" After a while, it became clear to Joan that she would never get any better. Joan and everyone else around her had to admit that. Her only hope for a better life was to find some way to make her weaknesses her strengths.

Please think about the meaning of Step Two:

I am coming to believe that Jesus Christ came in a human body, that He is here with me now in Spirit, and that He has the power to change my weaknesses into strengths.

What difference does this Step make? If it's the truth, it makes all the difference in the world. This Second Step invites you to relax about where you are at this point in your life. Don't force yourself to be something that you're not or to do something that isn't you. Don't force yourself to believe. Believing is something that comes from within you. It's a gift. It isn't something you push yourself to do. This Step is a reminder that you are who you are. Accept that.

At the same time, you can gradually move toward someone or something. You can come to believe by opening yourself up to God, yourself, and others. This Step says that you are "coming to believe that Jesus Christ came in a human body." Is that hard to believe?

The Step says "that He is here with me now in Spirit." If that's true, wouldn't that make a big difference in your life?

This Step also says that Jesus Christ has the power to change "weaknesses into strengths." Whoa! Is that possible? For hundreds of years, people who have called themselves Christians have been saying their weaknesses have been changed into strengths.

God's Word tells us that all these parts of Step Two are true.

WHAT THE BIBLE SAYS ABOUT STEP TWO

I am coming to believe that Jesus Christ came in a human body, that He is here with me now in Spirit, and that He has the power to change my weaknesses into strengths.

Choose one passage from the selections given and read it each day during the next week. Think about the passage by checking the statements that describe how you feel. Then write a few words about how this passage applies to you.

1. The author of the fourth book of the New Testament, the book of John, wrote these amazing words to describe the fact that God became a human person just like us:

The Word was made flesh, and He lived with us, and we saw His glory, the glory that is His as the only Son of God, full of grace and truth (John 1:14).

Jesus Christ came in a body like mine.

____ That is hard for me to believe.
____ I want to believe it but don't yet.
____ This idea is too much for me, but I'm open.
__X__ I believe it.
__X__ Jesus knows what it is like to live this life.
_X_ _sometimes it seeme. hard 2 accept &_
sometimes sometimes I question it.

2. This author of the first book of the New Testament quotes Jesus as He says His last words to His disciples before He goes back to be in heaven with His heavenly Father:

And know that I am with you always; even until the end of time (Matt. 28:20).

Jesus Christ is with me now in Spirit.

____ I never thought about it.
__X__ I've always believed this.
____ I want to learn more about this.

__X__ *sometimes I 4get & just 4get about him which is bad but it happens*

_____

3. The author of the book of Hebrews was doing his best to persuade the readers that Jesus Christ understands what it's like to be a human being. He wrote,

Jesus Christ understands our weaknesses, since He had the same temptations we do, though He never once gave way to them and sinned. So let us come boldly to God's throne and stay there, confident and eager to receive His mercy and to find grace to help us in our times of need (Heb. 4:15–16).

__X__ Jesus understands weakness.
__X__ He is available to help me through mine. I will call on Him.
__X__ Jesus Christ has the power to change my weaknesses into
__X__ strengths.
____ I need His help and all the help I can get.
____ I don't believe it. I feel like a hopeless cause.
____ I want to believe this, but I have no evidence.

____ _____
_____
_____

4. No one has ever made the promises that Jesus has made because He is the only one who is able to make good on His promises. Over and

over, Jesus made statements about Himself and promises that have
challenged people all through history. People have tested Him and His
word, and they have found Him to be trustworthy and true. Here is one
of His greatest invitations:

> **Come to Me all you who are tired from carrying heavy loads,
> and I will give you rest. Take My yoke and put it on you, and
> learn from Me, because I am gentle and humble in spirit; and
> you will find rest. For the yoke I will give you is easy, and the
> load I will put on you is not heavy** (Matt. 11:28–30).

___ I am tired. I need God's rest.
___ I will come to Him with my heavy load and take the load that He
has to give me.
___ I want to trust in Jesus' promise. God, help me.
___ I am willing to learn from Jesus. I am willing to take the load
that He gives me.

___ _____

_____

_____

Jesus asks, "What do you want Me to do for you?"
Read this passage twice each day in the next week:

As Jesus was getting close to Jericho, there was a blind man
sitting at the side of the road begging. He heard the crowd
passing by and asked what it was all about. And they told him,
"Jesus the Nazarene is going past you."

So the blind man shouted out, "Jesus, Son of David, have pity
on me!" The people in front scolded him and told him to keep
quiet, but he shouted all the louder, "Son of David, have pity on
me!" So Jesus stood quite still and ordered the man to be
brought to Him. And when he was quite close, He asked the
blind man, "What do you want Me to do for you?" "Sir," he
replied, "let me see again." Jesus said to him, "You can see
again! Your faith has saved you." And instantly his sight returned,
and he followed Him, praising God; and all the people who saw
it gave praise to God for what had happened (Luke 18:35–43).

Check these out...

1. Choose one or several. If I had been a blind person at the side of the road, I would have

    ____ been quiet and hoped Jesus would have noticed me.
    ____ yelled louder and more than the blind man did.
    ____ started swinging my fists at everyone who told me to shut up.

    ____ _____

2. When Jesus said, "Bring the blind man over here," how would you have felt if you were the blind man?

    ____ Relieved.
    ____ Snobbish. It'd be about time Jesus would identify the most important people.
    ____ Scared.
    ____ Humbled.
    ____ Embarrassed! Why did I create this scene?
    ____ Important! Jesus cares about me!

    ____ _____

3. When have you cried out to Jesus? Did others ever tell you to stop doing that? What was the situation?

    _____

    _____

    _____

    _____

4. If Jesus asked you the question, "What do you want Me to do for you?" how would you answer it?

    ____ I'd ask Him to help me in my relationship with my family, especially my _____.
    ____ I'd ask Him to give me one good friend.
    ____ I'd ask Him to help me stop this one bad habit.
    ____ I'd ask Him to take away my pain.
    ____ I'd want Him to leave me alone.

    ____ _____

Even though Joan, the girl who was paralyzed, was confined to her bed or her wheelchair, she began to use that weakness to her advantage. Two phones, which were donated by several charitable organizations, were installed in her room. One was for business use; the other for personal use. She was able to use those phones and her time to help others.

Everyone has weaknesses. Everyone has strengths. We really don't use our strengths as we could. Our weaknesses often hinder us. Alone, we can do little about them. But God can do great things!

Jesus Christ came in a human body like yours and mine. He had headaches and heartaches. He was lonely. He went through rejection. He was afraid.

He went through a growing-up process like we do. He was like us in every way except He did not sin. That's what makes Him different from anyone who ever lived. Jesus Christ was tempted, but He never sinned.

Jesus understands what life is like for us. He has been with us in human form. He is here with us now in Spirit. He knows everything we experience. He is with us in the process.

More than that, Jesus Christ has the power to change our weaknesses into strengths. Most people try to change themselves in their own power. For a while that works like a New Year's resolution. Most people lose their drive and discipline. They don't have the power to continue in their good intentions. They need Jesus Christ to help them make the necessary changes.

Finally, think about this story:

One Solitary Life

Here is a man who was born in an obscure village . . . the child of a peasant woman. He grew up in another obscure village . . . he worked in a carpenter shop until he was thirty . . . and then for three years he was an itinerant preacher.

He never wrote a book . . . he never held an office . . . he never owned a home . . . he never had a family . . . he never went to college . . . he never put his foot inside a big city . . . he never traveled more than two hundred miles from the place where he was born ... he never did one of the things that usually accompany greatness ... he had no credentials but himself ... he had nothing to do with this world except the naked power of his divine manhood. While still a young man, the tide of popular opinion turned against him ... his friends ran away. One of them denied him ... he was turned over to his enemies ... he went through the mockery of a trial ... he was nailed to a cross between two thieves ... his executioners gambled for the only piece of property he had on earth while he was dying ... and that was his coat.

When he was dead, he was taken down and laid in a borrowed grave through the pity of a friend.

Nineteen centuries have come and gone and today he is the centerpiece of the human race and the leader of the column of progress.

I am far within the mark when I say that all the armies that ever marched ... and all the navies that were built ... and all the parliaments that ever sat, and all the kings that ever reigned put together have not affected the life of people upon this earth as powerfully as has that One Solitary Life.

—Anonymous

MY REFLECTIONS ON STEP TWO

I am coming to believe that Jesus Christ came in a human body, that He is here with me now in Spirit, and that He has the power to change my weaknesses into strengths.

What do you think about Step Two? Write down your feelings, thoughts, and ideas.

_____

_____

_____

_____

_____

_____

_____

_____

For further study:

• John 3:1–8
• Colossians 1:15–20
• John 1:12–14
• John 3:16
• Romans 8

CHAPTER 3

I Put My Trust in Someone Greater Than Myself

Step Three:

*I turn my will and my life
over to Jesus Christ,
my Lord and Savior.*

PUTTING MY TRUST IN SOMEONE GREATER
THAN MYSELF

For several weeks I had been experiencing numbness and tingling on the left side of my body. I have generally been in good health. I am able to run three miles three times each week.

Suddenly, the pains and sensations came out of nowhere, and my doctor, after doing all the tests he could, sent me to a neurologist. The neurologist ordered an overwhelming series of tests. (I didn't know the body could be checked in so many ways.)

First in the series were numerous blood tests, all of which turned out to be negative. Those were followed by an EMG (this is a great one for kids who don't have enough excitement in their lives; it's a test that uses electrical jolts, shocks, and needles), a brain wave test, and two MRI's—a brain scan and neck scan.

Hard as the test was, I had a great experience with the EMG. The attending technician was one of the friendliest young ladies I had ever met.

After a brief explanation of the process that she was about to put me through, she said, "You can do this test. The Lord will be with you." That prompted me to ask if she was a Christian. "I've been a believer since 1980," she said, "but I've *really* been a believer since 1988."

"What happened then?" I asked.

"I was doing a test like I'm doing on you," she said as she stuck another needle in my thigh.

"The guy lying on this table had AIDS. He told us. Our whole office knew it. I was praying for him all the while I was administering the test. And then I did a crazy thing. I poked myself with a needle that I had just taken out of his arm. I have never done anything like that before in my whole career."

She hesitated for a few moments as tears rolled down her face. "For six months, we didn't know what the future of my life would be like. I was immediately put on a medication to counteract the HIV virus—a medication that really messed up my body. For six months, we had to wait to know for sure whether I had been infected with AIDS. My husband and I spent many nights on our knees. I totally surrendered my life to Jesus Christ. I gave Him everything I had. I learned to live one day at a time, and I'm still doing it."

As she finished the EMG test on me, she told me that up to this point she still tests negative.

Several days before the MRI tests, my wife, Nancy, and I were told about the two worst possibilities: (1) a malignant brain tumor (assuming they could in fact find a brain!) or (2) multiple sclerosis.

"Anything other than those two would be good news," Nancy said.

We both spent three nights "dreaming" (nightmaring) about what might happen should either be the diagnosis.

All we could do, with each thought, was surrender, turn my body over to Jesus Christ, and ask Him to do what must be done. I felt much liberation and freedom as I was able to let go of the outcome of the tests and the future of my life—even if that future meant major surgery or confinement to a wheelchair.

I had heard about the infamous MRI "tunnel" and how difficult it was for claustrophobic people. Fortunately, I was not one of those people. My body was small enough to fit comfortably into the tight space.

Inside the "tunnel" for the MRI brain scan, I realized how helpless I was. There was nothing I could do but lie there. All I could do was "let go." Let the technicians do what they needed to do; let the doctor do what he needed to do; all I could do was surrender and lie still. I survived the experience by imagining I was in the sleeping quarters of a great sailboat. I can tolerate anything that has sailing involved with it.

"The good news is, you have a brain, and it is fine," the neurologist reported three days after the test. "You have no tumor and no multiple sclerosis." He went on, "The bad news is, we still don't know what is causing these problems in your body, and so the testing will continue" (translated, the torture will continue).

After more tests the doctor discovered that I have three degenerating disks in my neck, and they have caused and will cause the pain, the numbness, and the tingling. I have had to stop running and have had to learn ways to live with this condition until or when I will need surgery (never, if I can do anything to avoid it).

Through this experience, I have again realized how terribly vulnerable and fragile I am. At any moment I could need surgery, be in a wheelchair, or face death. All are simple reminders that my life has lasting value only when it is committed to Jesus Christ and lived moment by moment for Him. He is using all of these daily experiences to draw me closer to Himself.

This is an example of a minor issue in my life. Many and more challenging trials have taken me back to the same place. If I am to enjoy life, I need to give it to Jesus Christ. I need to turn my fears over to Him.

Think about your own fears.

HOW ABOUT YOU?

Today, what are you most afraid of?

____ Heights

____ Water

____ Being alone

____ Being left out

____ That my parents might divorce

____ That I will be abused

____ Sickness

____ My parents

____ Flunking out of school

____ The future

____ That one of my parents will die

____ That I will abuse someone

____ _____

____ _____

____ _____

____ _____

Here are some fears other teens shared with a group. (Check the ones that also apply to you.)

____ "I'm trying to be myself when I don't know what myself is." *Eileen*

____ "The thing I am afraid of most right now is not being accepted by peers...or at least having them accept me as I am." *Julie*

____ "What I am most afraid of right now is facing the high-school life of drugs and alcohol." *Steve*

—— "I am most afraid of getting pregnant." *Laurie*

—— "I am afraid of adulthood the most. I have no idea of what I want to do or become. Getting a real job and becoming responsible are very frightening." *Tracy*

—— "I am afraid of failing in life and my parents being ashamed of me." *Jeff*

_____

_____

_____

Once we have identified our fears, we must decide how to overcome them. One way is to take Step Three: turn our lives over to Christ and allow Him to help us.

TAKING STEP THREE

When I was in parochial grade school, I was often challenged by the sisters who taught me. Sometimes I felt encouraged to turn my will and my life over to God because of the modeling that they did for me. Most times I didn't even think about turning my life over.

As I look back at those experiences, I think that what held me back was fear. I was convinced that if I gave my life to God, I would have to do three things: give up everything I had ever liked, become a priest, and go to Africa!

I have since learned this important truth: God's will for my life will bring me joy. When I am doing His will, I will be enjoying life the most.

I have given my life and my will to Jesus Christ. I'm not a priest. I have not been to Africa (yet), although I've been invited several times, and my life has not been miserable because I had to give up everything I have ever liked. In fact, my life has been as rich as it could be. Jesus Christ promises full lives to those who give their lives to God. All those who turn their lives over to Him experience His promises as the truth.

I will admit that I have learned a great deal about giving up things that have seemed important to me. What has it been like for you to give up things? In comparison, what has Jesus given to you?

JESUS' DISCIPLES TRUSTED HIM WITH THEIR LIVES

Read this each day this week:

One day Jesus got into a boat with His disciples and said to them, "Let's go across to the other side of the lake." They began their journey. As they were sailing, Jesus fell asleep. Suddenly a strong wind blew down on the lake, and the boat began to fill with water. They were all in great danger. The disciples went to Jesus and woke Him up, saying, "Master, Master, we are about to die." Jesus got up and gave an order to the wind and to the stormy water; they quieted down, and there was a great calm. Then He said to the disciples, "Where is your faith?" But they were amazed and afraid, and said to one another, "Who is this person? He gives orders to the wind and waves, and they obey him" (Luke 8:22–25).

Check these out . . .

1. What is your favorite kind of boat?

____ Powerboat
____ Sailboat
____ Fishing boat
____ Canoe
____ No boat
____ A boat sitting safely on shore

2. What is your favorite body of water?

____ Lake (*name*) _____

____ Ocean (*name*) _____

____ River (*name*) _____

____ Pond _____

3. If you had been in the boat with Jesus and the disciples, what might you have done?

____ Kept sailing, trusting that I'd get to the other side without Jesus' help.

——— Stayed out of the boat to begin with. I know when storms are coming.

——— Bailed out when the storm hit.

——— Called Jesus much earlier.

4. What is the most difficult "storm" you have ever been "caught" in? (*For instance, I was in a big fight with my little brother, and my mom came home.*)

_____

_____

_____

5. Who helped you in that storm? (*For instance, she stopped us both from hurting each other.*)

_____

_____

_____

6. In what ways has Jesus saved you? (*For instance, he has saved me from doing something harmful to my little brother.*)

_____

_____

_____

Step Three, turning our lives over to Jesus, is a hard step. God has given us freedom—freedom to choose. This Step, in one sense, asks us to give that freedom back to God. It asks us to give control of our lives back to Him. To surrender. To let go. To let God work in and through us. To let Him be Lord.

This Step asks us to trust. Specifically, it asks us to trust Jesus Christ. This Step asks us to give Him our wills and our lives. Our wills are our decision-making abilities. Our lives are everything else: our feelings, friends, possessions, problems, ideas, dreams, pain, and this moment.

It is a choice that we make freely and deliberately. It is a choice that we make in stages. The more we get to know Jesus Christ, the more we trust Him and give Him of ourselves. Jesus doesn't force us to do this—He invites us.

This Step may feel a bit scary. There's really nothing to be afraid of. Jesus Christ is the kindest, most gentle, and most loving person history has ever known. He can be trusted.

This Step is important because a lot is at stake here. You may decide not to turn your will and life over to Jesus. That means you have decided that you will continue to be your own savior.

God does love you. He does have a plan for you. His plan for you is rich and full. When you turn yourself over to your Creator, your life is fulfilling. If you hold back, you may be missing out on the great things that God has in store for you. Consider what the Bible says about taking Step Three.

WHAT THE BIBLE SAYS ABOUT STEP THREE

I turn my will and my life over to Jesus Christ, my Lord and Savior.

Choose one passage from the selections given and read it each day during the next week. Think about the passage by checking the statements that describe how you feel. Then write a few words about how this passage applies to you.

1. John, the author of the gospel of John, is also the author of the book of Revelation. In this book, the last book of the New Testament, John describes a vision of Jesus coming to speak to all churches and all individuals. In this case, He is coming to the church of Laodicea, a church that Jesus says is "neither hot nor cold."

Jesus says, "Listen, I stand at the door and knock; if anyone hears My voice and opens the door, I will come into your house and eat with you, and you will eat with Me" (Rev. 3:20).

____ I am like that church in Laodicea. I am neither hot nor cold about all this stuff.

____ Jesus, I know that only I can open the door to my heart. I hear You knocking.

____ Jesus, I open my heart, will, and life to You. Please come in.

—— _____

—— _____

—— _____

2. Written by Solomon, recognized as the wisest king who ever lived, these verses instruct us to depend on God and not on our own abilities:

> **Trust in the Lord with all your heart. Never rely on what you think you know. Remember the Lord in everything you do, and you will be shown the right way. Never let yourself think that you are wiser than you are; simply obey the Lord and refuse to do wrong** (Prov. 3:5–7).

—— God, help me to trust in You.
—— God, help me to obey You.
—— God, forgive me for wanting to do life on my own. Help me to turn my will and my life over to You, Lord Jesus.

—— _____

—— _____

—— _____

Write your thoughts and feelings after reading these passages.

1. When I think of turning my will and my life over to Jesus Christ, I feel *(for instance, relief: I know this is the best thing I can do; God, help me to trust in You; help me to obey You)*

_____

_____

_____

2. List the names of all the people you know who have been hurt, harmed, or disappointed by Jesus when they have turned their lives over to Him.

_____

3. Indicate where you are with this Step:

    ____ I didn't know that Jesus wants my life.
    ____ I have given Him my will.
    ____ I have given Him my life.
    ____ I don't understand how to do this.
    ____ I'm interested but scared.
    ____ I don't know where I am with this Step.

4. Today, what part of you is holding back from turning your will and life over to Jesus Christ? (For example, I'm not ready. I don't know enough about this.)

    _____

    _____

    _____

5. What does it mean to have Jesus as your Savior? Savior from what? Savior for what? (For example, Jesus will save me from a bad life. He will eventually take me home to heaven. While I am here, He wants me to help others.)

    _____

    _____

    _____

    _____

6. Now think about the fears you identified at the beginning of this chapter. Frame a plan for dealing with any of these problems if it really happened. (For instance, I am afraid of the future. I can do several things to change that. I can pray for God's guidance; trust God to lead me and guide me; talk to my parents or see a counselor about my future; do research and get prepared for the future and my career; enjoy every day I have and just relax about the future.)

    Your fear: _____

    Your plan: _____

    _____

    _____

_____

_____

_____

Your fear: _____

_____

Your plan: _____

_____

_____

_____

_____

Your fear: _____

_____

Your plan: _____

_____

_____

_____

_____

Ask Jesus to make Himself and His plan known to you. Your life will become more directed, and you will become more like Him. When you turn your will and life over to Jesus, you will know peace.

The first part of the following prayer, the Serenity Prayer, is used at most Alcoholics Anonymous meetings. I have adapted and included the whole prayer, the first and second parts as they have been written.

Begin to turn your life over to Christ by saying this prayer in the morning and/or evening each day this week.

The Serenity Prayer

God,
grant me the serenity to
accept the things I cannot change,
courage to change the things I can, and
wisdom to know the difference.
Living one day at a time,
enjoying one moment at a time,
accepting hardship as a pathway to peace,
taking as Jesus did,
this sinful world as it is,
not as I would have it,
trusting that You will
make all things right
as I surrender to Your will,
so that I may be reasonably happy
in this life and supremely happy with You
forever in the next.

—Reinhold Niebuhr

MY REFLECTIONS ON STEP THREE

I turn my will and my life over to Jesus Christ, my Lord and Savior.

What do you think about Step Three? Write down your feelings, thoughts, and ideas.

_____

_____

_____

_____

_____

_____

_____

_____

_____

_____

Exercise: Turn over as much of your will and your life as you possibly can to Jesus Christ right now. Ask God to help you let go.

For further study:
- Luke 15:11–32
- 1 Peter 5:7–9
- 1 John 4:15–17
- 1 John 5:4–5, 11–13

CHAPTER 4

I Discover All of Me

Step Four:

I begin honestly listing what I know and discover about myself: my strengths, weaknesses, and behavior.

I DISCOVER ALL OF ME

"One of the reasons I think I keep comparing myself to other kids is that I don't know who I am. I don't know what makes me different. So being with other kids always makes me feel smaller than them," Tim, a tenth grader said. "Maybe if I knew myself better, I would feel better about myself."

Tim was fifteen years old. He was the youngest of five children. All his life he had been compared to his older brothers and sisters. They had all done well in school. He was sick of being known as the "little brother."

All his life his performance had been compared to the performance of his older brothers and sisters. He learned how to do that to himself; all that seemed to matter to him was how well he could do and whether he could do it better or faster than anybody else. Instead of appreciating himself, he was always putting himself down—comparing himself to others and always feeling like they did everything better than he did.

He had great grades in English but did poorly in math. Instead of feeling good about the English, he was constantly beating himself up about how stupid he was in math. He seldom gave himself praise, and most of the time he was upset with how poorly he was doing about everything. That was the pattern of his life.

Tim was never happy being Tim. He always had to be working on making himself better.

Finally, through these Steps, Tim is learning to like himself just as he is. He is learning how to quit comparing himself to others. He is having more fun now because he can relax. He doesn't feel like he has to impress anybody. He is impressed with himself just as he is.

Step Four is about getting to know yourself better. This Step will help you like and love yourself as you are. But you can't love someone or something you don't know. When you know yourself, you will feel more secure, directed, and defined.

For some people, the idea of doing this Step is scary. I suppose part of the reason why some people get afraid is that this Step encourages them to spend some time alone. When did you last take the time to be alone so that you could hear what your heart wants to say to you? Take a moment now and do the following warm-up exercise to begin to get to know yourself.

WARM-UP FOR STEP FOUR

Write down the first things that come to your mind.

My favorite color: _____

My favorite food: _____

My favorite animal and why: _____

_____

My favorite room in the house: _____

My best time of the day: _____

What I like to wear most: _____

My two best friends right now: _____

_____

My favorite place in the world: _____

The best treat anyone could ever give me: _____

_____

My favorite holiday: _____

Three words my friends would use to describe me:

He/she is _____

He/she is _____

He/she is _____

Three things I want to be someday *(for instance, hockey player, coach, artist, mother, teacher):*

1. _____

2. _____

3. _____

Three things I have been *(for instance, Boy Scout/Girl Scout, basketball forward, altar boy, artist):*

1. _____

2. _____

3. _____

Three things I need to say to myself:

1. _____

2. _____

3. _____

When I first took a Step Four inventory, I thought about my entire life—the physical, emotional, and spiritual parts. I also looked in the Bible to see how God described me. Take a moment now to see yourself as God sees you.

WHO YOU ARE IN GOD'S EYES

1. David the giant killer and great king of Israel talked to God often in the Psalms. This is the picture God gave him of himself:

> **You, O God, created every part of me. You put me together in my mother's womb. I praise You because You are to be feared. Everything You do is strange and wonderful. I know it with all my heart.**

> **When my bones were being formed and carefully put together in my mother's womb, when I was growing there in secret, You knew that I was there; You saw me before I was born. The days given to me had all been recorded in Your book before any of them ever began** (Ps. 139:13–16).

When I realize that God created me and is involved with my life right now, I feel

    ———— scared.
    ———— embarrassed.
    ———— excited.
    ———— relieved.

———— ——————————————————————————————

—————————————————————————————————

—————————————————————————————————

When I first realized that God made me, I was overwhelmed. He made me. I am not an accident, it's true. I have a purpose in this life. I have a reason for being here. When I forget these important truths, I get messed up, and I forget them when I don't take time to remember them.

God not only made me; He is still very involved in my life. He is with me at all times. I need to take the time to hear Him remind me about that.

2. Paul wrote these words to a group of Christians to remind them how important and valuable they are in God's eyes:

We are God's work of art, created in Jesus Christ (Eph. 2:10).

When I read what St. Paul wrote about me, that I am a "work of art,"

    ———— I don't believe it.
    ———— I don't care. So what else is new?
    ———— I am grateful for the reminder.
    ———— I believe it and get excited about it.

———— ——————————————————————————————

—————————————————————————————————

—————————————————————————————————

3. Jesus wants people to know who they are. He wants people to know what their gifts are. He wants people to have the joy of using their gifts to help others. He said,

People don't light a lamp and then hide it or put it under a bowl; instead, they put it on the lampstand so that others may see the light as they come in (Luke 11:33).

When Jesus said, "Don't light a lamp and then hide it," what that means to me is:

____ I need to use my gifts and talents.
____ Get fired up.
____ Get my lamp, light it, and let others see the real me.
____ I need to get busy finding out where the lamp and the light are.
____ I don't know what that means.

____ _____

_____

_____

When I first understood that God gave me gifts, I became quietly excited. God has given me gifts to share with others. He has given me talents. I have something to offer others.

These are just a few of the discoveries I have made as I have done this Fourth Step. In the next few pages you will find several suggestions on how you can go about discovering more about yourself.

TAKING STEP FOUR

Getting to know yourself is a lifelong process. Bit by bit, day by day, you can get a better understanding of who you are. In Step Four, you will clearly and specifically write down what you know and discover about yourself. Step Four also helps you learn more about your life story.

When you do Step Four, begin with now. Begin with the facts you know are true: you are loved, gifted, cared for, and created with a purpose, and other things you know about yourself.

Accept yourself as you are. Enjoy who you are.

This Fourth Step is an inventory. That means you count or list your strengths and weaknesses. Step Four also asks you to be aware of some of the things you do—your behavior.

A STEP FOUR INVENTORY

The best way to do this Step is to do only a section at a time. Please don't try to do the whole inventory at once. Do as much as you can in one week, then move on to the other Steps. When you remember something about yourself, and you don't have your book with you, write it on a piece of paper, bring that discovery to your book, and enter it in this section.

You can work on this Step while you continue to go through the other Steps.

List your strengths and weaknesses. The following pages will help you get started. Add something to the list each day or week.

1. Who Am I Now?

What do I really like? *(For instance, cats, music, trips, favorite jeans, favorite food.)*

_____

_____

_____

_____

_____

_____

What do I really dislike? *(For instance, cats, being alone, being with other people, school.)*

_____

_____

_____

_____

_____

_____

What encourages me most? *(For instance, good grades, a phone call from my best friend, music, my church group.)*

_____

_____

_____

_____

_____

_____

What discourages me most? *(For instance, when certain kids don't like me, being lied to by a friend, being left out.)*

_____

_____

_____

_____

_____

_____

What are my strengths? *(For instance, I am a good reader; I can ski well; I care about people; I am not afraid to try new things.)*

_____

_____

_____

_____

_____

_____

What are my weaknesses? *(For instance, I can be a really selfish person; I get upset easily with my little brother; I think only about what I want.)*

_____

_____

_____

_____

_____

_____

Here are some weaknesses that other teens expressed when they took their Step Four inventories. (Check those that also apply to you.)

_____ "The biggest mistake I ever made was lying or not letting my feelings out." _Carol_

_____ "The biggest mistake I ever made was to get involved with boys." _Marilyn_

_____ "The biggest mistake I ever made was doing drugs because they messed up my life." _William_

_____ "My biggest mistake was not showing my feelings and telling someone how I felt about them." _David_

_____ "The biggest mistake I've ever made was thinking the popular group had all I ever needed and letting them rule my life. Now I want real friends, and they won't let me go." _Jill_

_____ "My biggest mistake is continuing to do things I know I would regret with people I would not even want to communicate with later in life." _Catherine_

Some things I like about my body _(for instance, I like my hair; I like the color of my eyes; I like how healthy my body is)_:

_____

_____

_____

_____

_____

_____

_____

Some things I like about my mind and the way I think *(for example, I am smart; I can read fast; I can remember things)*:

_____

_____

_____

_____

_____

_____

Some things I like about my personality *(for example, I like how friendly I can be; I like people; I am funny; I can make others feel better about themselves)*:

_____

_____

_____

_____

_____

_____

Some things that I can really do well *(for example, ski, Roller-blade,® swim, sing, play an instrument, write stories, have fun)*:

_____

_____

_____

_____

_____

_____

A few things I know I'm not good at *(for instance, cleaning my room, doing my homework, writing school papers, saving my money, listening to my parents)*:

_____

_____

_____

_____

_____

_____

What I feel I want to do with my life in the future (for example, make lots of money, help poor people, be a missionary, live in the country, have five kids):

_____

_____

_____

_____

_____

Some of my dreams (for example, I dream of someday living on a sailboat, sailing from one port to the next; I have a dream of someday being a professional baseball player; I dream of going to college):

_____

_____

_____

_____

_____

My three most urgent unanswered questions (for example, why did God let my friend die? Why does my dad [mom] drink so much? Why did my parents get a divorce?):

1. _____

_____

_____

2. _____

_____

_____

3. _____

_____

_____

Some people and things have helped make me the way I am now.

Write about your dad, mom, brothers, sisters, and other influential family members. *(For instance, my grandparents were always there for me when I came home from school. They listened to me as I described my day in school.)*

_____

_____

_____

_____

_____

_____

How I feel about myself (check one, several, or all):

___ I feel loved as I am.

___ I feel I'm a good person.

___ I feel I'm a bad person.

___ I feel I need to do things faster than others to be loved.

___ I feel I need to be perfect to be loved.

___ I feel I need to be stronger than others to be loved.

___ I'm okay just as I am. I don't need to change a thing.

___ All the changes I need to make are very minor.

___ It's not okay to feel. I have to hide what I feel.

___ I need to work harder to be loved.

___ If I want to be loved by others, I need to please them.

___ It's wrong for me to think about myself and what I want and need out of life.

—— I'm important.

—— I'm not important until I do something really big.

My feelings about my schools, teachers, and classmates (one-sentence reactions):

Ages 1–5 *(for instance, I felt loved and wanted)*:

_____

_____

Ages 6–9 *(for instance, this period of life is kind of a blank)*:

_____

_____

Ages 10–12 *(for instance, I have good feelings about my uncle who spent a lot of time with me)*:

_____

_____

Junior high *(for example, fear, lonely, turmoil, insecure about dating)*:

_____

_____

Senior high *(for example, searching, unsettled)*:

_____

_____

Other important stuff about who I am now:

_____

_____

_____

_____

_____

_____

_____

_____

_____

_____

2. Who Am I in Jesus?

Here's another very important part of doing Step Four: discovering more about who you are now because of Jesus Christ. Look up each passage listed. After reading each one, write a few words that describe who you are in Christ.

In this passage Paul tells us who we are and how we got to be that way:

> **If anyone is in a relationship with Jesus Christ, that person is a *new creation*. The old has passed away, and the new has come. All this is from God who called us back to Himself and gave us the gift of eternal life** (2 Cor. 5:17–18).

In Christ, I am _____

This is one of the most essential verses in the Bible. In just a few words John tells the best news the world has ever heard:

> **For God so *loved* the world that He gave His one and only Son so that everyone who believes in Him will not die but have eternal life** (John 3:16).

In Christ, I am _____

Jesus gives us a gift no one else is capable of giving. Only Jesus can give us what we really want.

> **"You will know the truth," Jesus says, "and the truth will set you free. I am the way, the truth, and the life. If I set you *free*, you will truly be free"** (John 8:32; 14:6).

In Christ, I am _____

Paul helps us define who we are by listing several major qualities that God has given us. After you've read the passage, list the words that describe who you are. Paul writes,

> Blessed be the God and Father of our Lord Jesus Christ, who has **blessed us with all the spiritual blessings of heaven** in Christ.
>
> Before the world was made, He **chose us** in Christ, to be **holy, spotless,** and to **live in His presence.** We have become His **adopted** sons and daughters, chosen from the beginning, through Jesus Christ, **for His own kind purposes.** He gives us **freedom** and the **forgiveness** of our sins.
>
> He has **let us know the mystery** of His purpose...that He will bring everything together under Christ.
>
> **We have heard** the message of the truth and the good news of our salvation and **have believed** it.
>
> We have been given the faith to **put our hope in Christ,** and we have been **stamped with the seal of the Holy Spirit** (Eph. 1:3–14).

In Christ, I am _____

_____

_____

_____

_____

_____

_____

3. What Do My Actions Say About Me?

The last part of Step Four is about behavior, what you do or don't do. Briefly answer the questions.

Am I using my gifts? ___ yes   ___ no

How? (*For instance, I am doing my best to help my friends in school. When I know they are having problems, I go to them and let them know that I am available to listen to them.)*

_____

_____

_____

_____

Am I working on my weaknesses? ___ yes   ___ no

How? *(For instance, I am trying to be patient with my little brother rather than blow up whenever he talks to me.)*

_____

_____

_____

What am I doing that I should not be doing?

_____

_____

_____

What am I not doing that I should be doing?

_____

_____

_____

What are my addictions right now?

_____

_____

_____

_____

_____

_____

WHAT THE BIBLE SAYS ABOUT STEP FOUR

I begin honestly listing what I know and discover about myself: my strengths, weaknesses, and behavior.

Choose one passage from the selections given and read it each day during the next week. Think about the passage by checking the statements that describe how you feel. Then write a few words about how this passage applies to you.

1. This passage is taken from a letter that the prophet Jeremiah sent to the people who followed God. They were very discouraged because they were living in a land that was not their own. They had been taken to the country by pagans. Jeremiah wrote this passage to remind them that God is in control:

I alone know the plans I have for you, plans to bring prosperity and not disaster, plans to bring about the future you hope for (Jer. 29:11).

—— I believe God has great plans for me.
—— I will surrender my heart, mind, and will to Him so that He can accomplish His plans in and through me.
—— I need God's help in believing He has a plan for me.
—— I need God's help in doing God's plan for me.

—— _____
_____
_____

2. In both of these passages, Paul gives convincing evidence that each one of us has been given a gift or gifts and that each one of us is an important person:

Each one of us has received a special gift according to what Christ has given. The Spirit's presence is shown in some way in each person for the good of all (Eph. 4:7; 1 Cor. 12:27).

—— I am not convinced I have any special gifts.
—— I need to discover my gifts.

___ I know I have a special gift to share with others.
___ This is exciting news. I will share myself with others.

___ _____

_____

_____

3. God will help us if we are sincerely seeking understanding about our gifts, Paul says in this passage. He declares,

Now instead of the spirit of the world, we have been given the Spirit that comes from God, to teach us to understand the gifts that we have been given (1 Cor. 2:12).

___ I don't understand this at all. I need help.
___ God has given me the Holy Spirit who will teach me what my gifts are and how to use them.
___ I am open to being taught about this.

___ _____

_____

_____

4. Timothy was probably about seventeen years old when he was called to be a disciple of Jesus Christ. Paul was his teacher and mentor. He wrote to remind Timothy that his youth didn't matter. What mattered was that he was gifted. Paul urged him to use his gift:

Fan into a flame the gift that God gave you when I laid my hands on you. God's gift is not a spirit of fear, but the Spirit of power, love, and self-control (2 Tim. 1:6–7).

___ Because I am young, I sometimes feel I have nothing to give to others.
___ God has given me a gift or gifts. I need to use and express these gifts right now.
___ I will not be timid in using or sharing these gifts.

___ _____

_____

_____

Each day that you work through your Step Four inventory, you might say the following prayer:

A Fourth Step Prayer

Dear Lord Jesus,

I don't want to kid myself. I want to know who I really am. Even though I am afraid of this some of the time, I really do want to know myself better.

I know I have strengths and weaknesses. That's the way my life is now. I'm sure that's the way it will always be. Help me to be okay with that.

Help me to believe that You love me as I am. Help me to love myself as I am. Help me to love others as they are.

Please give me an understanding of my gifts and talents so that I may properly use them to have a full life and help others in the process.

Thank You, Lord Jesus.

MY REFLECTIONS ON STEP FOUR

I begin honestly listing what I know and discover about myself: my strengths, weaknesses, and behavior.

What do you think about Step Four? Write down your feelings, thoughts, and ideas.

_____

_____

_____

_____

_____

_____

_____

_____

_____

_____

Exercise: Today, begin your lists for Step Four.

For further study:

• Galatians 5
• Romans 12
• Colossians 3:5–17
• John 8:34–36

CHAPTER 5

I Share My Life with True Friends

Step Five:

I am ready to honestly share with God and another person the exact nature of my strengths, weaknesses, and behavior.

TRUE FRIENDS

David seemed to be a shy person. His schoolmates hardly noticed him. He never volunteered an answer or a comment in any class. After school, he "disappeared." He never went to any games or social activities at school. He was a loner.

He seemed nice enough but a little mysterious. The girls thought he was attractive but had no real way of knowing whether he was a good kid or not.

David gave the impression that he had plenty of friends and that he didn't need anybody for anything. The truth was, David had no friends and only a few acquaintances. He was playing a game with himself and others.

If there had been a suicide in David's school, everyone would have guessed that David had done it.

In his senior year in high school, David was invited to participate in a church group ski trip. One of the sharper guys in the class had decided to make David his "project" for the year.

To everyone's surprise, David accepted the invitation, went on the trip, and had a great time. Eventually, David became active in the youth group. The other kids in the group welcomed him.

The more acceptance he felt from the other kids, the more he expressed himself and his true feelings. As they shared their lives with him, he began to open up and share his.

His story was not that unusual. But every time David talked, you could see how much impact his family's moves and his parents' divorce had on him. He resented having to move three times. He loved and missed his dad. He was angry that he couldn't be with him more. As David became more active in his group, he shared those feelings, and he became much healthier.

David has encouraged other kids to share more of their lives. They have learned that the more real stuff they share, the more they will love and respect one another.

TAKING STEP FIVE

The Fifth Step helps you begin this type of sharing. This Step urges you to let another person, or several persons, see the real you. Basically, that's what all of us are looking for. We want to know others, and we want them to know us.

Yet our culture has not taught us how to relate. We have been so impressed with TV, movies, videos, and electronic games, we very seldom sit down and talk with others about what life is really like for us. Step Five helps us to shut down on the technology and invites us to get into real life.

Begin sharing your real feelings with one other person. Then share some of your feelings with a group of kids. You will change, and so will they.

All kids have the same desires:

• To have at least one deep, long-term friend.
• To be known for who they really are by another person.
• To know at least one other person as that person really is.

The Fourth Step reminds us to list what we know about ourselves. The goal is to try to get to know ourselves (our strengths and our weaknesses) better.

Step Five urges us to share what we have discovered with God and with another person. This Step urges us to come clean about who we are. It challenges us to look at what we do and maybe change some of what we do. We may even need to break away from a habit or from friends who are not good for us.

Let's look at what the Bible says about taking Step Five.

WHAT THE BIBLE SAYS ABOUT STEP FIVE

I am ready to honestly share with God and another person the exact nature of my strengths, weaknesses, and behavior.

Choose one passage from the selections given and read it each day during the next week. Think about the passage by checking the statements that describe how you feel. Then write a few words about how this passage applies to you.

1. John urges us to be honest with ourselves and God:

If we say we have no sin in us, we are kidding ourselves and refusing to admit the truth; but if we freely admit that we have sinned, then God who is faithful and just will forgive our sins and make us thoroughly clean from all that is evil (1 John 1:9–10).

2. James offers practical advice if we want to be healthy:

Get into the habit of admitting your sins to each other and praying for each other (James 5:16).

I'm most anxious about sharing myself honestly with

___ God.
___ myself.
___ another person.

In sharing myself with another person, I'm mostly afraid of

___ being criticized.
___ being condemned.
___ being known for who I really am.
___ being rejected.
___ being judged.

___ _____

If I tell someone else who I really am, I believe the person

___ will hate me.
___ will think less of me.
___ will understand.

___ _____

Have you ever really tried letting someone else know the real you?

_____ yes   _____ no

What was it like?

_____

_____

_____

Think of one person with whom you'd like to share your Fifth Step. Are you willing to make a commitment (to yourself or to your group) to set up an appointment to see this person?

The person's
name: _____

_____ yes   _____ no

_____ I will call this person tomorrow.

PEGGY'S STORY

Peggy was a tenth grader when she went on a weekend retreat with her youth group. She had no idea the retreat would have as much impact on her as it did. She loved being there. She was overwhelmed with the love that adults and other kids had for her. The retreat experience opened her up to share more of her life.

She said, "I lived a lie most of my life. I ran away from myself and some of the things that I did. I denied so many things about myself and what I did. Finally, I admitted my sin to Jesus. I felt His forgiveness. Then I talked to my best friend. I could trust her. I knew I could. After talking with her, I got up enough courage to go see my pastor. I told her all about me. Everything. It felt so good to let it all come out . . . to tell the truth. I am so glad and thankful that I did it."

No one can explain the wonderful freedom that comes to us when we tell the truth to ourselves, God, and another person. The relief is beyond description when we discover that we are still loved even though we've done and continue to do some strange things, and when we discover that others have the same feelings, fears, and ideas.

Admitting to ourselves, God, and another person means there is no more hiding, lying, or denying. Admitting means that we have looked squarely into the mirror and that we know who we are and we accept that.

As we talk all this over with God, we will find the forgiveness, peace, and power that we need to live fuller, healthier, and cleaner lives.

Sharing ourselves with a group leader, pastor, counselor, teacher, or trusted older friend will help us to find the freedom we need to change our behavior.

MY REFLECTIONS ON STEP FIVE

I am ready to honestly share with God and another person the exact nature of my strengths, weaknesses and behavior.

What do you think about Step Five? Write down your feelings, thoughts, and ideas.

_____

_____

_____

_____

_____

_____

_____

_____

_____

_____

Exercise: Today, confess your sins to Jesus. Admit them. Let Him forgive you and cleanse you completely as He promised.

For further study:

• Psalm 32:1–5
• John 3:19–21
• John 1:29–34
• 1 John 5:11–13

CHAPTER 6

I Want My Life to Be Different

Step Six:

*I am entirely ready to have
Jesus Christ heal all
those areas of my life
that need His touch.*

I WANT MY LIFE TO BE DIFFERENT

Carol was a cute girl who was best known for her great attitude. She was always smiling and cheering others up.

She had a steady boyfriend. They didn't seem to be too serious, but everyone knew that they were going steady. They had been going out for about two years when suddenly John wanted to get out of the relationship.

Carol went into a tailspin. She hadn't realized that her whole life had revolved around John and his life. She had basically cut herself off from her best girlfriends. She hadn't participated in afterschool stuff.

Her life had become a small world. It had spun down to John and her. And now John was gone.

For months she tried to pull herself out of the slump. Nothing seemed to work. She lost her positive attitude. She wasn't pleasant to be around. Most kids forgot what the real Carol was like.

Because everyone pulled away from Carol, she didn't have friends to let her know how she was coming across to others. Her self-esteem was sinking quickly.

Carol tried several other boyfriends. She used them and found they weren't capable of taking care of her need. Carol knew that she had a blank spot in her life. She finally admitted that the blank spot had been there ever since she could remember. It was a lonely and dark place that seemed to be right in the center of her heart.

For years, she had done things to impress other people. She was sure they would like her if she could accomplish great things. And she did. She was great on the piano. She played in the band. She was on the oral interpretation team. And she still maintained a B average.

When John came along, he would be the person who would fill the blank spot, Carol thought. So she let herself get totally wrapped up in him. She even compromised her morals to please him. She thought she could keep him if she did everything he wanted to do.

Now John was gone. And now, for the first time, Carol was facing the truth about herself. She was fed up with all the things she had done to please and impress others. She wanted people to like and respect her for who she was, not for what she could do.

Carol was ready for the Sixth Step. Without doubt, she was ready to be changed, and she knew she couldn't do the changing. She needed Jesus' help to do that. She knew enough about Jesus to know that He would be there for her. All she needed to do was to call out for His help.

LET GO AND LET GOD

People hurt. People have areas of their lives that they want changed. They get fed up with the hurt and those parts of their lives that need to be changed. One day, finally, they get fed up enough to say, "This is it. I give up. I am entirely ready for something different in my life. I've had it. I want to be healed and changed. I don't want to live like this any longer." For a while they try to do this changing on their own.

Step Six is another step that reminds us to let go . . . to surrender . . . to give up fighting and trying to change on our own. Jesus comes to us to say, "Let Me touch you. Let Me heal you."

Being entirely ready brings freedom and liberation. It's important to be ready, entirely ready, or little progress and few changes will happen.

Jesus has been called the great Healer. Here is yet another story of someone He healed.

The Woman Who Was Bent Double

One Sabbath day He was teaching in one of the synagogues, and a woman was there who had been ill for eighteen years. She was bent over double and was quite unable to straighten herself up.

When Jesus noticed her, He called her and said, "You are set free from your illness!" And He put His hands upon her, and at once she stood upright and praised God (Luke 13:10–13).

1. Check the statements that are true about this woman.

    ____ She was eighteen years old.
    ____ She was bent over double.
    ____ She was a champion tennis player.
    ____ She was unable to straighten up.
    ____ Jesus came to her home.
    ____ Jesus told her she would be set free from her illness.
    ____ Jesus put His hands on her.
    ____ She praised God.

2. Check the statements that are true about you.

    ____ I am a champion tennis player.
    ____ I am bent over double.
    ____ I have a pain/problem that has been with me a long time.
    ____ I am entirely ready to have Jesus touch me and make my life different.
    ____ I want to be entirely ready, but I don't know how.
    ____ Ready for what? I don't understand.

3. When Jesus said, "You are free from your illness,"

    ____ He meant, "Straighten up, lady, and then I'll help you with your illness."
    ____ He meant what He said.
    ____ the woman had to stay doubled over until she said she was sorry for everything she ever did wrong (repent).
    ____ Jesus touched her and healed her because He loved her, and He didn't expect anything in return from her.

HOW ABOUT YOU?

We have to do our part if we want to grow, get healthier, and have fuller lives.

The woman's part was to

• know what her hurt was.

• get ready to have the hurt healed.

• get to the place and person who could do the healing.

Jesus' part was to

• respond to her pain.

Jesus always responds; however, He does it in His own time and His own way, not ours. When He saw the woman, He could have ignored her and permitted her to keep her illness.

He did that with Paul, you know. When Paul asked God three times to take the thorn from his side, God did not remove the thorn but told him that God's grace would be enough to get him through the hard times. In other words, for Paul, it was best for him that his illness—the thorn—be kept in his life (2 Cor. 12:7–10).

Jesus chose not to do it that way with the woman. Instead, He chose to heal her completely and instantly. He laid His hands on her.

If you want healing, your part is to

- get ready. (Identify your areas of need, hurt, and desired changes—Steps Four and Five.)
- get set. Be willing to let Jesus do the healing.
- go! Go to the person who can heal you—Jesus.
- let go. Put yourself and your concerns onto Jesus, and then let Him do what is best for you from His viewpoint.

1. List the most important changes that you want to take place in your life.

   Here are a few changes that other teens mentioned when they took Step Six.

   - "If I could change one thing in my life right now, it would be my introvertedness. I want to be more outgoing so I can relate to people better instead of just sitting back and watching." *Jane*
   - "The area in my life that needs to be changed is my temper towards teachers. I get mad too easily." *Dave*
   - "If I could change one thing in my life right now, it would be my personality." *Brigitte*

   a) _____

   b) _____

   c) _____

   d) _____

2. What is your part in bringing about these changes?

a) The change I seek *(for instance, to become more outgoing):*

_____

_____

What I can do about it *(for instance, talk to others, talk to my family about this):*

_____

_____

b) The change I seek *(for instance, hang around with different friends):*

_____

_____

What I can do about it *(for instance, go to my youth group and get to know the kids there):*

_____

_____

c) The change I seek *(for instance, get rid of my temper):*

_____

_____

What I can do about it *(for instance, apologize to those I've hurt and ask them to help me with my temper):*

_____

_____

d) The change I seek *(for instance, a change in my personality—I am too selfish):*

_____

_____

_____

What I can do about it *(for instance, begin thinking more about other people and what life is like for them)*:

_____

_____

3. What are you asking Jesus to do about these areas of your life (His part)?

a) *(For instance, Jesus, please help me to reach out to others. Give me courage to talk to other people.)*

_____

_____

_____

_____

b) *(For instance, Jesus, I know I need to be hanging around with a different group of kids. I'm fed up with this group. Please lead me to other kids that I can be friends with.)*

_____

_____

_____

_____

c) *(For instance, Jesus, please take my temper away.)*

_____

_____

_____

_____

d) *(For instance, Jesus, help me to concentrate on other people and how I might be helpful to them. Help me to take my mind off myself.)*

_____

_____

_____

_____

4. Look over your lists on Step Four. What part of your life most needs the touch of Jesus? _(For instance, I am tired of being lonely; Jesus, please come and take my loneliness away.)_

_____

_____

_____

_____

_____

5. What else needs to happen before you'll be entirely ready for Jesus to touch and heal you? _(For instance, before I will really stop judging others, one or two things will have to happen: [1] God will answer my prayer and help me, or [2] I will lose my friends.)_

_____

_____

_____

TAKING STEP SIX

Can your friends or an adult help you make these changes?

____ yes   ____ no

If so, who? _____

_____

_____

How? _____

_____

_____

____ I will talk to this person tomorrow.

All of us need help. All of us need to be touched by Jesus. Some of us are more aware of this need than others. We become more aware through painful experiences in life. We realize that we are not going to live forever. We realize that certain parts of our personalities need to change or we'll never get anywhere in life.

We know that we are not careful about our relationship with God. We are not listening to Him and obeying Him. Will it take a crisis in our lives before we will be ready for Him to come to touch and heal us? Will we have to hit bottom before we will let Jesus embrace us?

Step Six urges us to be entirely ready, to let go of things that would prevent us from freely and totally trusting Jesus Christ as Carol ultimately did.

MY REFLECTIONS ON STEP SIX

I am entirely ready to have Jesus Christ heal all those areas of my life that need His touch.

What do you think about Step Six? Write down your feelings, thoughts, and ideas.

_____

_____

_____

_____

_____

_____

_____

_____

_____

_____

_____

For further study:

- Ephesians 2:3–8
- Matthew 19:26
- Galatians 4:1–11, 5:1
- Acts 3:19–20

CHAPTER 7

I Ask for My Life to Be Different

Step Seven:

I humbly ask Jesus Christ to change my weaknesses into strengths so that I will become more like Him.

I ASK FOR MY LIFE TO BE DIFFERENT

Carol, the teenager in the last chapter who became disgusted with her behavior and attitude, finally hit bottom.

Her life came apart, one part after another, until finally she could not take things anymore. She lost her closest friends because she was hard to be with and she never called them.

She crawled into a shell and lived in her own little world. She ignored the fact that there were real people outside "her world."

Her grades steadily fell until she got to the point that she lost confidence in herself and her mental abilities.

Her behavior affected all of her family relationships. At one time, she had a good relationship with both her mom and her dad. Now, she never talked to them. All she did was grunt when someone asked a specific question. Her brothers quit trying to talk with her.

Carol was miserable.

She was ready to call out to God for help. Her experiences taught her that she was not capable of solving her problems and living life on her own. Her experiences humbled her and persuaded her that she needed God's help in her life.

A humble person is aware of his or her shortcomings and weaknesses. That was an unexplored area of Carol's life. She had never really thought much about her weaknesses. She admitted that she had been a proud person—she was not willing to acknowledge her weaknesses to herself or to others.

A humble person does not expect to be served. Humble people are pleasant to be with and often encourage others to be humble by their example.

Step Seven humbly asks Jesus Christ to touch us. Jesus Christ was humble. No other person was God in a human body, and yet He did not assume His position of power. He lowered Himself to become like us in all ways, except sin.

To humbly ask means to know our condition. We know our need. We know our weaknesses and limitations. And we are convinced we can do little to change our situation on our own. To humbly ask means to ask without assuming that God will answer our prayers (as if He is our errand boy). When we ask humbly, we are ready to receive and accept God's answer—whatever it may be.

To humbly ask means to rely on Jesus' power, the Holy Spirit within us, to change us. The Bible calls us to change our weaknesses into strengths through the power of the Holy Spirit.

Carol admitted her need for God. She finally cried out to Jesus and let Him know how much she needed Him. He came to meet her need. He pulled her out of her slump and gave her a new life.

Carol is now her old self—a self based on Jesus Christ and His way of life.

WHAT THE BIBLE SAYS ABOUT STEP SEVEN

I humbly ask Jesus Christ to change my weaknesses into strengths so that I will become more like Him.

Read the passage below each day during the next week. Think about the passage by checking the statements that describe how you feel. Then write a few words about how this passage applies to you.

In this straightforward list, Paul tells his friends in Colossae what they need to do to "clean up their act" if they want to become more like Jesus:

> **Now, you of all people must give all these things up: getting angry, being bad-tempered, spitefulness, abusive language, and dirty talk; and never tell each other lies. You have stripped off your old behavior with your old self, and you have put on a new self, which will progress toward true knowledge the more it is renewed in the image of its Creator (Col. 3:7–10)**

___ God, help me to do what this passage says I need to do.
___ Jesus, please strip off my old behavior and replace it with my new self, which comes from You.
___ Lord Jesus, help me to become more like You.

___ _____

_____

_____

TAKING STEP SEVEN

1. Identify one part of your life that you know needs healing. Here are some examples of what other teens said when they thought about changing their lives.

   • "If I could change one thing in my life, it would be my feelings of insecurity." *Tammy*
   • "It's really hard for me to meet the expectations of my family and friends . . . to be able to do everything my school and friends want me to do." *Jack*
   • "Right now I'm afraid to change and try new things. I'm scared I'm going to die, not ever find someone to love, messing up my life with drugs." *Carol*

   _____

   _____

   _____

2. Have you ever asked Jesus to heal a part of your life before?

   ___ yes   ___ no

   What was it like? (For instance, *I asked Jesus to give me a better attitude toward this one kid in school, and He did it; I asked Jesus to take away my loneliness, and He did it.*)

   _____

   _____

   _____

3. I want to become more like Jesus.

—— Not really.

—— Kinda. It would be fun to walk on water.

—— It's impossible for me. I don't have a chance of ever becoming more like Jesus.

—— I'm going to ask Him to change me so that I can become more like Him.

4. Read the following from the apostle Paul:

> **With your eyes wide open to the mercies of God, I ask you, my dear brothers and sisters, to worship God by giving Him your bodies as a living sacrifice, consecrated to Him and acceptable by Him.**
>
> **Don't let the world around you squeeze you into its own way of doing things, but let God change you into His own mold ... by changing your mind from within** (Rom. 12:1–2).

When I read this passage, I

—— want to worship God by giving Him my body as a living sacrifice.

—— regret that I have let the world squeeze me into its own way of doing things.

—— want God to change me by changing my mind from within.

—— _____

_____

_____

Only Jesus Christ and the Holy Spirit can make these changes. Our role is to ask and to ask humbly. He is Lord. He will answer in His own way and in His own time. When we humbly ask, we are ready to accept whatever He will give us or withhold from us.

THE POWER OF THE HOLY SPIRIT

Several Bible passages discuss the person and work of the Holy Spirit. These passages help us discover the transforming power and the enabling that the Holy Spirit gives us as we humbly ask Jesus Christ to change our weaknesses into strengths. We will look at three of them. You might want to read the others when you work through the Twelve Steps again.

1. Jesus said that the Holy Spirit is a gift we receive. Our role is to ask. He declared,

> **If you then, who are evil, know how to give your children what is good, how much more will the heavenly Father give the Holy Spirit to those who ask Him** (Luke 11:13).

____ I don't know what to make of this passage.

____ This has happened to me. I have asked for the Holy Spirit. He has come. He has filled me with Himself.

____ I didn't know I had to ask. I just thought the Holy Spirit automatically came to live in my heart and help me for life.

____ I want the Holy Spirit. I am asking the Father to give Him to me.

____ _____

_____

_____

2. Paul reminds us that the Holy Spirit comes into our lives and hearts and brings evidence that we are God's children:

> **The proof that you are God's children is that God has sent the Spirit of His Son, Jesus, into our hearts: The Spirit that cries, "Abba [Daddy], Father," and it is this that makes you a son or daughter...and an heir** (Gal. 4:6–7).

____ I would like this kind of proof.

____ God has sent the Spirit of His Son into my heart.

____ God is my Father (Daddy). I am His son/daughter.

_____

_____

_____

3. After His death and resurrection, Jesus instructed His disciples to stay in Jerusalem and wait for the power of the Holy Spirit to come

upon them. When the Holy Spirit comes into our lives, He fills us with power—the kind of power that we need to change our lives. Jesus said,

> **You will receive power when the Holy Spirit comes on you, and then you will be My witnesses . . . to the end of the earth** (Acts 1:8).

____ I need this power to change my life.
____ I am afraid of this power.
____ I need all the help I can get. My life needs to be changed.
____ I'm open to the power and work of the Holy Spirit.

____ _____

_____

_____

Here are the other passages that talk about the power of the Holy Spirit:

- John 7:37–39
- John 14:12–16
- John 14:17
- John 14:26
- Acts 2:4
- Acts 2:15–17
- Acts 8:14–18
- Acts 10:45–46
- Acts 19:1–7
- 1 Corinthians 1:4–9
- 1 Corinthians 12 (especially verse 3)
- 1 Corinthians 14 (especially verses 1–5)
- Galatians 5:22
- 1 John 2:10
- 1 John 2:27

Lord Jesus

Through all of these Steps, I come to You with a better understanding of my strengths, weaknesses, shortcomings, and gifts, and also with my sin. I know I have sinned, Lord. Please forgive me. Please do more than forgive me. Please change me so that I will become more like You. I come now to the point where I really need You, probably as I never have before. Please change my weaknesses into strengths. I know through the power of Your Holy Spirit, You will change me.

When I want to criticize, help me to see good things in others.

When I want to lie, help me to be honest.

When I want to hate, help me to love.

When I want to judge others, have mercy on me, and give me that same mercy for others.

When I want to do wrong, help me to do right.

Lord, please change me. Please take away my bad habits. Replace them with good ones. Please change my heart. Please change my mind. Please change my attitude.

I promise to do my part—to change what I can. But I know that only You have the power to change me and make me like Yourself.

I pray that You would do all this, Lord Jesus, in Your name.

MY REFLECTIONS ON STEP SEVEN

I humbly ask Jesus Christ to change my weaknesses into strengths so that I will become more like Him.

Write a letter to God. Humbly ask Him to change your weaknesses into strengths.

Dear God:

_____

_____

_____

_____

_____

_____

_____

_____

_____

_____

_____

_____

Your friend,

_____

For further study:
- John 4:43–54
- Psalm 51:1–13
- Matthew 18:1–4

CHAPTER 8

Give Me the Guts to Mend the Relationship

Step Eight:

I make a list of the people I have hurt and become willing to go to them to mend the relationship.

GIVE ME THE GUTS TO MEND THE RELATIONSHIP

Brad and Josh were juniors in high school. Both were starters on the varsity football team. They were in the same middle school, junior high school, and now high school. Ever since Brad could remember, he was in competition with Josh. Brad felt that he always had to be on his guard whenever Josh was around. Josh was good at putting Brad down by saying embarrassing things in front of other teammates. Because Brad was quieter and not as quick with his mouth, he always left encounters angry and frustrated.

It got to the point that the two of them were constantly bickering and badgering each other. Things got very serious between them when Brad started a false rumor about Josh. The lie spread throughout the school, and Josh was very embarrassed.

"I'm gonna kill you," Josh said to Brad every time he saw him in the hallway. "You deserve to die for telling people lies."

Brad was afraid of Josh. He knew he had done wrong, but he didn't know how to fix the situation. He decided to see one of the youth directors from a local church, a guy who dropped by the school often.

"What can I do?" Brad asked Rob, the youth leader.

"If it were me," Rob said, "I'd go back to Josh, tell him you did start the rumor, and tell him you're sorry."

It took a great deal of courage for Brad to call Josh on the phone and apologize. Surprisingly, Josh accepted Brad's apology. It may be hard to believe, but they became really good friends after all that.

Brad's willingness broke the ice and created the possibility of beginning a new relationship.

Unfortunately, making amends doesn't always go so well. Many kids who have tried to make amends were rejected and hurt. Their attempts to restore the relationship were rebuffed.

The important thing is for us to do our part by acknowledging what we've done wrong, admitting it to ourselves and God, and then being willing to go to the person to make amends.

You may be familiar with this Bible passage: "So then, if you are bringing your offering to the altar and there remembering that your brother has something against you, leave your offering there before the altar, go and be reconciled with your brother first and then come back and present your offering" (Matt. 5:23–24). Step Eight is another way of reminding us that we need to be reconciled with our "brothers and sisters."

Step Eight is as old as Bible times. One tax collector named Zacchaeus took this Step hundreds of years ago.

The Tax Collector Makes Amends

Then Jesus came into Jericho and was making His way through it. There He found a wealthy man called Zacchaeus, a chief tax collector, wanting to see what sort of person Jesus was. But the crowd prevented him from doing so, for he was very short. So he ran ahead and climbed up into a sycamore tree to get a view of Jesus as He was heading that way. When Jesus reached the spot, He looked up and saw the man and said, "Zacchaeus, hurry up and come down. I must be your guest today." So Zacchaeus hurriedly climbed down and gladly welcomed Him. But those standing by muttered their disapproval, saying, "Now Jesus has gone to stay with a real sinner." But Zacchaeus himself stopped and said to the Lord, "Look, Sir, I will give half my property to the poor. And if I have cheated anybody out of anything, I will pay him back four times as much." Jesus said to him, "Salvation has come to this house today. It is the lost that I came to seek and to save" (Luke 19:1–10).

1. Why do you think Zacchaeus was so anxious to see Jesus?

    ＿＿ He had everything else in life, and he needed some excitement.

    ＿＿ He did a Fourth Step with the Jericho Twelve-Step group and decided it was time to have his life changed.

___ His life was empty.
___ He saw the need for Jesus in his life.

2. Jesus came for the

___ rich and famous.
___ short and funny.
___ lost.
___ religious people.

3. Zacchaeus's first vocal response to Jesus was,

___ "I will give half my property to the poor."
___ "If I have cheated anybody out of anything, I will pay him back ten times."
___ "I never hurt anybody."
___ "I didn't do anything wrong."

4. Pretend you are Zacchaeus. You have met Jesus, and He has invited Himself to your house for lunch. What is your reaction as He invites Himself?

_____

_____

_____

How does His invitation make you feel?

_____

_____

_____

Does Jesus' presence remind you of the need to make amends (as it did for Zacchaeus)?

___ yes   ___ no

Do you sense Jesus' love for you?   ___ yes   ___ no

Do you feel ready to make amends because God has come to visit you and let you know that He accepts you as you are?

___ yes   ___ no

TAKING STEP EIGHT

There are two major parts to Step Eight:

1. Making a list of the people whom we have hurt—the people we will make amends with.
2. Making a list of the people who have hurt us—the people we will forgive.

Making Amends with Those I have Hurt

Make your list of people you have harmed. Begin with those you have hurt today. Gradually work your way back into time so that you include those you have hurt this past week, this month, this year.

Open yourself up to be reminded of someone you hurt quite a while ago. Maybe it was a lie that you told, a rumor that you started. Perhaps you stole something. Maybe you insulted a family member or a teacher.

Look again at your list of behaviors in Step Four. Have you done something wrong to another person? The purpose of Step Eight is to mend the relationship with that person so that you can be free and the relationship can continue.

Nothing is more vital than relationships. It is especially important to keep the ones that we have. Our relationships, especially ones with the family, are God's greatest gifts to us. Everything else in life—including material things—means nothing in comparison to our friendships and relationships. That's why it's so essential to be sure that our relationships are "together," mended, united.

Making this list may not feel good, but it is the right thing to do. It will take courage, but it will set us free. We all have a need to be set free, to make amends, to have a clean slate. We all need the peace and relief that come with knowing that our relationships have been restored.

My list of those I have hurt and with whom I want to mend a relationship includes the following people.

Family:

_____

_____

_____

Friends:

_____

_____

_____

Relatives:

_____

_____

_____

Teachers:

_____

_____

_____

Pastors:

_____

_____

_____

Others:

_____

_____

_____

Making Amends with Those Who Have Hurt Me

Most people have at least one unreconciled relationship in their lives. As a person who is in a relationship with Jesus Christ, I know that I am loved and forgiven. I have the freedom to love and forgive others. I can take the initiative to mend the relationship, even if I am convinced I have not been the one responsible for breaking the relationship to begin with. No matter what the outcome of my going to make amends might be, I will always have Jesus Christ with me.

Reconciliation is of the highest priority. It doesn't matter who was right or who was wrong. As a Christian, I have the responsibility to make the move to reconcile.

And Jesus tells us how to do it. If your brother or sister does something wrong, He says, go and have it out between yourselves. If he or she listens to you, you have won that person back. If she or he does not listen, take one or two others along with you: the evidence of two or three witnesses is required to sustain any charge. But if she or he refuses to listen to them, report it to the community, and if he or she refuses to listen to the community, treat that person like a pagan or a tax collector (Matt. 18:15–17).

1. What is your experience with this passage?

       ____ I've never heard of such a thing.
       ____ This makes sense to me.
       ____ I have had this done to me; this process has worked for me.
       ____ I have done this with someone else. It really works.
       ____ I don't understand.
       ____ I'm willing to give this a try.

       ____ _____

       _____

2. To what degree are you willing to use this approach right now with your family and friends?

       ____ I think it's a good idea, but I don't think it's for me.
       ____ This seems like a scary way to do it.
       ____ I avoid arguments at all costs. I'm getting out of this situation.
       ____ I need practice in doing this. I know it's right, but I've never done it.
       ____ I don't understand.

       ____ _____

Now make a second list. Identify the people who have hurt you.

Ways in which I have hurt myself:

       _____

       _____

_____

_____

Family members who have hurt me:

_____

_____

_____

Friends who have hurt me:

_____

_____

_____

_____

Relatives who have hurt me:

_____

_____

_____

_____

Teachers who have hurt me:

_____

_____

_____

_____

Pastors who have hurt me:

_____

_____

_____

_____

Others who have hurt me:

_____

_____

_____

_____

What the Bible Says About Step Eight

Forgiveness is not easy. Without Jesus' help it seems impossible. Let's look at what He said about forgiveness.

Please read the following passages and select a response that most describes where you are right now.

1. Jesus gave His disciples teaching that they had never heard before. He spoke with authority. They listened. Perhaps His most difficult teaching was this one, which is important as we think about those who have hurt us.

Jesus says, "Love your enemies, do good to those who hate you, bless those who curse you, and pray for those who mistreat you (Luke 6:27–28 NIV).

____ Without Your help, Lord Jesus, I cannot go back to those who have hurt me.

____ I need to make amends.

____ This is impossible for me to do. I want to, but I cannot pray for or go to those who have mistreated me.

____ I can't do this yet, but I can clearly identify those who have hurt me.

____ _____

_____

_____

2. In response to their expressed desire to pray, Jesus taught the disciples a pattern for prayer. Here is a portion of what is now called the Lord's Prayer:

Forgive us our debts, as we also have forgiven our debtors. And lead us not into temptation, but deliver us from the evil one. For if you forgive men when they sin against you, your heavenly Father will also forgive you. But if you do not forgive men their sins, your Father will not forgive your sins (Matt. 6:12–15 NIV).

___ I need God's forgiveness.
___ I need God's help in forgiving others.
___ I think I live dangerously if I do not forgive others.

___ _____
   _____
   _____

3. Solomon, a wise king in the Old Testament, wrote most of the book of Proverbs. Listen to his words:

Do not say, "I'll pay you back for this wrong!" Wait for the Lord, and He will deliver you. Do not say, "I'll do to him as he has done to me; I'll pay that person back for what he did" (Prov. 20:22; 24:29).

___ These passages help me with my feelings of revenge (my feelings of wanting to get even).
___ I am learning to let the Lord "deliver" me.
___ I will let the Lord pay back a person who has wronged me. God will do what is right.

___ _____
   _____
   _____

4. Part of loving one another is being sure that the relationship is reconciled and "together." People are looking for this unity. This unity is evidence that we are His disciples.

Jesus says, "A new command I give you: Love one another. As I have loved you, so you must love one another. By this all

people will know that you are My disciples, if you love one another" (John 13:34–35).

_____ To love my brother and sister means I am reconciled with them.
_____ If I love them, I will do what I can to make amends.
_____ By the love we have for one another, the world will know we are Christ's disciples. I believe this.

_____ _____
_____
_____

Strange as it may seem, most people begin the work of Step Eight by making amends with themselves. They gently recognize areas of their lives where they have hurt themselves. For some that means acknowledging they have been too hard on themselves, expecting too much and depriving themselves of a great deal. For others, that means realizing they have not lived life with honesty.

MY REFLECTIONS ON STEP EIGHT

I make a list of the people I have hurt and become willing to go to them to mend the relationship.

What do you think about Step Eight? Write down your feelings, thoughts, and ideas.

_____
_____
_____
_____
_____
_____
_____
_____
_____

For further study:
- Luke 6:31
- Matthew 5:20–48
- 1 John 4:11–12
- Matthew 6:14–15
- 1 Peter 4:7–8
- Ephesians 4:32

CHAPTER 9

Friends Again

Step Nine:

*I make amends with the people
I have hurt, except when to
do so might bring harm
to them or others.*

FRIENDS AGAIN

Recently, the principal called a high-school student out of class. Someone from the family was waiting in the principal's office. As the student entered, he knew that something very serious had happened. He was right. His father had been killed suddenly in a car accident just a few hours before. The son was overwhelmed. He loved his father dearly. Both father and son were very well known and liked in the school.

In no time the news spread throughout the school. An unusual thing happened during every break between classes for the rest of that day. At each break, kids were lined up at every available telephone. They were calling their dads to let them know they loved them.

Step Nine reminds us of the urgency in going to people to express our love and concern. Don't hesitate. The importance of being reunited with others cannot be overemphasized. The need is indescribable. Nothing can surpass the wonderful feelings of having restored relationships, of being reconciled.

One young man, long ago, had the courage to take Step Nine. He returned to his home to make amends. You might have heard him called the prodigal son.

The Prodigal Son

Once there was a man who had two sons. The younger one said to his father, "Father, give me my share of the property that will come to me in my inheritance." So the father divided up his property between the two sons.

Before very long, the younger son collected all his belongings and went off to a foreign land, where he wasted his wealth in wild living.

When he had run through all his money, a terrible famine arose in that country, and he began to feel the pinch. Then he went and hired himself out to one of the citizens of that country, who sent him out into the fields to feed the pigs. He got to the point of longing to stuff himself with pig food, but not a person would offer him anything.

Then he came to his senses and cried aloud, "Dozens of my father's hired men have more food than they can eat, and here I am dying of hunger! I will get up and go back to my father, and I will say to him, 'Father, I have done wrong in the sight of heaven and in your eyes. I don't deserve to be called your son anymore. Please take me on as one of your hired men.'"

So he got up and went to his father. But while he was still some distance off, his father saw him and his heart went out to him, and he ran to embrace him. But his son said, "Father, I have done wrong in the sight of heaven and in your eyes. I don't deserve to be called your son anymore."

"Hurry," called out his father to the servants. "Get the best clothes and put them on him! Put a ring on his finger and shoes on his feet. Get that calf we've fattened and kill it, and we'll have a feast and a celebration! For this is my son. I thought he was dead, and he's alive again. I thought I had lost him and he's found!" And they began the festivities (Luke 15:11–24).

1. In this story, I feel that

    —— I am like the son, returning to ask forgiveness and to make amends.

    —— I am like the father, waiting for someone to return home to make amends.

    —— I am like neither person; I can't relate to this story.

—— _____

_____

_____

2. The main thing I get out of this story right now is this:

____ Don't ask for your inheritance when you are young.
____ Jesus is like the father.
____ The father forgave the son and was waiting for him to return.
____ I want to go "home" to get things straightened out.

____ _____

_____

_____

3. The hardest thing about going to make amends for me is

____ making up my mind whether I should go.
____ making the first move to go.
____ going.

____ _____

_____

_____

4. What holds me back from making amends is this feeling:

____ I fear rejection.
____ I fear punishment.
____ It's not worth it.
____ It's no big deal. I really don't need to go.

____ _____

_____

_____

5. For just a few moments, pretend you are the son who returns home after wasting his inheritance. What are your feelings as you are walking toward your home and you see your father stepping out to meet you? Write about them.

_____

_____

_____

_____

As people involved in the Twelve Steps, our part is to go to those people with whom we need to restore a relationship. We have to express our feelings, our apologies, our sorrow about the broken relationship. Sometimes we need to ask forgiveness. We always need to forgive them for what they have done (or not done) to us before we go to them.

Don't expect anything from them. Their response is their response—you cannot control it. It would be best if they accept your apology. In some cases, they may not. You can't do anything about that. They may reject you. That is the risk you will take. However, you will be at peace inside because you did everything you could to improve the relationship.

TAKING STEP NINE

Think about the list you made in Step Eight. On this list, which three persons have you hurt the most?

1. Name: _____

   Nature of how the relationship was hurt:

   _____

   _____

   _____

   Verbal amend: _____

   Is a more substantial amend necessary? ___ yes   ___ no

   If so, what should it be? _____

   _____

   Commit to a time and place when you will meet with this person to take steps toward restoration and healing.

2. Name: _____

   Nature of how the relationship was hurt:

   _____

   _____

   Verbal amend: _____

   Is a more substantial amend necessary? ___ yes   ___ no

If so, what should it be? _____

_____

Commit to a time and place when you will meet with this person to take steps toward restoration and healing.

3. Name: _____

Nature of how the relationship was hurt:

_____

_____

Verbal amend: _____

Is a more substantial amend necessary? ___ yes   ___ no

If so, what should it be? _____

_____

Commit to a time and place when you will meet this person to take steps toward restoration and healing.

Before you meet with them, think about what the Bible says about Step Nine.

WHAT THE BIBLE SAYS ABOUT STEP NINE

I make amends with the people I have hurt, except when to do so might bring harm to them or others.

Choose one passage from the selections given and read it each day during the next week. Think about the passage by checking the statements that describe how you feel. Then write a few words about how this passage applies to you.

1. Jesus gave us a new commandment. It is not an option. We cannot choose to do it if we feel like it.

Jesus says, "I give you a new commandment: love one another, just as I have loved you, you also must love one another. By this love you have one for another, everyone will know that you are My followers (John 13:33–34).

—— Most of the time, loving others comes pretty easy for me.

—— This is my call, to love others.

—— One of the best ways that I can love others is to make amends with them.

—— Today, I pray for the willingness to do that.

—— _____

_____

_____

2. Paul informs us about one of our roles in life:

Therefore, if anyone is in Christ, that person is a new creation; the old has gone; the new has come! All this is from God, who reconciled us to Himself through Christ and *gave us the ministry of reconciliation* that God was reconciling the world to Himself in Christ, not counting men's sins against them. And He has committed to us the message of reconciliation. We are therefore Christ's ambassadors, as though God were making His appeal through us. We implore you on Christ's behalf: Be reconciled to God (2 Cor. 5:17–20).

—— God has made me a new creation by calling me into a relationship with Himself.

—— I know that He has now given me the privilege of being a friend maker for Him.

—— He is appealing to others through me, urging them to be reconciled to God and to one another.

—— I haven't thought about this very much.

—— _____

_____

_____

Step Nine gives us an excuse to go to others. Usually, our strongest and best relationships are the ones that have had a reconciliation, ones where the two parties have come back together after a time of disagreement, like Brad and Josh. Use this Ninth Step as your reason to get closer to the people from whom you have been separated.

MY REFLECTIONS ON STEP NINE

I make amends with the people I have hurt, except when to do so might bring harm to them or others.

What do you think about Step Nine? Write down your feelings, thoughts, and ideas.

_____

_____

_____

_____

_____

_____

_____

_____

_____

Exercise: Today I will go to the first person on my list. I will go, call, or write to make amends.

For further study:
- Romans 13:7–8
- Matthew 5:43–48
- Matthew 6:12
- 1 Peter 3:9
- 2 Corinthians 5:17–19

CHAPTER 10

My Daily Checkup

Step Ten:

Each day I do a review of myself and my activities. When I am wrong, I quickly admit it. When I am right, I thank God for the guidance.

MY DAILY CHECKUP

I went to parochial (private) schools for grade school and high school. I remember vividly those important days. I'll never forget the hard oak desks and beautifully polished hard oak floors. Specifically, I remember the blackboards in our classrooms.

In grade school, the blackboards were used frequently. By the end of the day, the boards were mostly white. One student would stay after school to clean them with wet rags.

When we returned to school in the morning, the boards were clean. We had fresh boards to work with. The clean boards made me feel good and fresh. I felt as if I could start a new day with a clean slate.

We need to clean our personal boards every day. Our hearts and minds need a daily cleansing, just like our bodies do. If I want to live a peaceful life with freedom from guilt, I have to learn how to do a daily review. I have to learn how to close the door to one day so I can open the door to a new day.

Doing a daily review or inventory is a matter of habit. It is a way of life. It is a great way to use the natural rhythm and cycle of daily life to remind us to stay close to God, ourselves, and others. This style of life keeps us fresh and reconciled. Step Ten helps prevent the "stockpiling" of anxiety, sin, and broken relationships.

Step Ten is a healthy step. All by itself, Step Ten could do much to make us healthier and happier. The apostles advised the early Christians to take Step Ten. Let's look at what the Bible says about taking a daily inventory.

WHAT THE BIBLE SAYS ABOUT STEP TEN

Each day I do a review of myself and my activities. When I am wrong, I quickly admit it. When I am right, I thank God for the guidance.

Choose one passage from the selections given and read it each day during the next week. Think about the passage by checking the statements that describe how you feel. Then write a few words about how this passage applies to you.

1. The apostle Paul offered the Galatian Christians this advice:

Each one should test his own actions. Then he can take pride in himself, without comparing himself to somebody else (Gal. 6:4 NIV).

_____ I want to take pride in myself.
_____ I want to test my own actions and nobody else's.
_____ I am responsible for my own behavior and the assessment of that behavior.
_____ I need not be concerned with others—what they do or what they think of me.

_____ _____

_____

_____

2. The apostle Paul told the Ephesians not to let the sun go down on their anger:

Be made new in the attitude of your minds; and . . . put on the new self, created to be like God in true righteousness and holiness. Therefore each of you must put off falsehood and speak truthfully to his neighbor, for we are all members of one body. "In your anger do not sin": Do not let the sun go down while you are still angry, and do not give the devil a foothold. He who has been stealing must steal no longer, but must work, doing something useful with his own hands, that he may have something to share with those in need. Do not let any unwholesome talk come out of your mouths, but only what is helpful

for building others up according to their needs, that it may benefit those who listen. And do not grieve the Holy Spirit of God, with whom you were sealed for the day of redemption. Get rid of all bitterness, rage and anger, brawling and slander, along with every form of malice. Be kind and compassionate to one another, forgiving one another, just as in Christ God forgave you (Eph. 4:23–32 NIV).

____ As I read this passage, I am convinced of the importance of keeping a clean slate day by day.
____ This passage reminds me of the importance of getting things settled before I go to bed at night.
____ I will use this passage as a checklist to help me in my evaluation of the day.
____ This passage will be especially helpful in assessing what I have said throughout the day.

____ _____
_____
_____

3. And the apostle James gave specific instructions about how they should live their daily lives:

Everyone should be quick to listen, slow to speak, and slow to become angry, for man's anger does not bring about the good life that God desires. Get rid of all that is wrong in your life, both inside and outside, and accept the word planted in you, which can save you. Do not merely listen to the word, and so then kid yourselves. Do what it says. Anyone who listens to the word but does not do what it says is like a man who looks at his face in a mirror and, after looking at himself, goes away and immediately forgets what he looks like. But the man who looks intently into the perfect law that gives freedom, and continues to do this, not forgetting what he has heard, but doing it—he will be blessed in what he does. If anyone considers himself religious and yet does not keep a tight rein on his tongue, he deceives himself, and his religion is worthless (James 1:19–26).

—— This passage is important for me because _____
_____
_____

—— I want to but don't know how to do this passage.
—— The true test of how well I am doing is whether I am being obedient to God and what He tells me in His Word.
—— I want to listen to and act on what He tells me.

—— _____
—— _____
—— _____

When I am wrong, I generally

—— deny it.
—— avoid it.
—— pretend it didn't happen.
—— admit it.
—— find someone else to blame.
—— ask for forgiveness.

The idea of doing a daily review of myself and my activities seems

—— tedious; I really don't have the time for it.
—— terrific; I've done it for years. It's the only way to live.
—— exciting, but I don't know how to do it.
—— to be a great idea, but I know myself well enough to know I'll never do it without some help and encouragement.
—— like something I want to develop.

Why not try Step Ten this week?

TAKING STEP TEN

Each day I do a review of myself and my activities. When I am wrong, I quickly admit it. When I am right, I thank God for the guidance.

A Daily Inventory

Taking a daily review or doing a daily inventory is simple. It is a matter of spending the last few minutes of the day reflecting on what that day was like. Use the form to help you get started.

Jesus gave us four simple and basic principles that are the ultimate test of whether we are living rich and full lives. These are some of the greatest passages from the Bible. All daily reviews must include these principles.

Jesus said,

1. **You must love the Lord your God with all your heart, with all your soul, and with all your mind** (Matt. 22:37).
2. **You must love your neighbor as yourself** (Matt. 22:39).
3. **You must love your enemies** (Matt. 5:44).
4. **You must pray for those who persecute you** (Matt. 5:44).

One way to do a daily review is to look at these four passages and ask yourself, *How have I done each of these principles today?*

Another way to do a daily review is to look at what Paul has written in two of his letters. Both are great daily review resources.

Paul wrote a "love letter" to the Corinthians (1 Cor. 13:4–8). You've probably heard it read at weddings. Now you can use it for a daily review of your life.

____ Today, have I been patient?
____ Today, have I been kind?
____ Today, have I been jealous?
____ Today, have I been boastful or conceited?
____ Today, have I been rude or selfish?
____ Today, have I taken offense or been resentful?
____ Today, have I taken pleasure in other people's sins or misfortunes?
____ Today, have I delighted in the truth?
____ Today, did I trust God and others?
____ Today, did I express hope?
____ Today, did I endure what came my way?
____ Today, did I love without conditions?

In his letter to the Galatians, Paul listed what he called the "fruit of the Spirit" (5:22–23). They are to be evidence that a person is a Christian. Use them on a daily basis to evaluate your life.

____ Today, have I been loving?
____ Today, have I been filled with joy?
____ Today, have I been at peace?

—— Today, have I been patient?
—— Today, have I been kind?
—— Today, have I demonstrated goodness?
—— Today, have I been trustful?
—— Today, have I been gentle?
—— Today, have I demonstrated self-control?

No human is capable of having or doing all of these. We all need Jesus Christ to come into our lives. We need Him to take over our hearts and lives, and to give us hearts that will be able to do all these important things. When we receive Jesus Christ, He gives us the ability to do what He asks of us. He wouldn't ask us to do something that we're not capable of doing. With Him living inside us, we can do all things; He gives us the ability to love, to pray, and to give of ourselves.

As our relationship with Jesus grows, our ability to love also grows. The more we get to know His love for us, the more we can love other people around us, even if they don't love us in return.

In light of the passages from the Bible on the previous pages, use the form below to help you with your daily review.

1. Recall the most important people that you have been with or spoken with throughout this day in sequence.

    The person: _____

    The event: _____

    The person: _____

    The event: _____

    The person: _____

    The event: _____

    The person: _____

    The event: _____

2. Ask God to forgive you if you have been at fault in any of these events with any of these people.

3. Forgive others if they were at fault in these events.

4. If you need to make amends in any of these situations, do so.

   Person's name: _____

   I will make amends right now or make a plan to do so tomorrow.

   ____ yes   ____ no

   Person's name: _____

   I will make amends right now or make a plan to do so tomorrow.

   ____ yes   ____ no

   Person's name: _____

   I will make amends right now or make a plan to do so tomorrow.

   ____ yes   ____ no

   Person's name: _____

   I will make amends right now or make a plan to do so tomorrow.

   ____ yes   ____ no

5. Thank God for the good things that have happened today and the guidance that He has given.

   Lord, I thank You for

   _____

   Lord, I thank You for

   _____

   Lord, I thank You for

   _____

   Lord, I thank You for

   _____

6. Close the door to the day. Forgive and forget. Give thanks for another day of life. Read the Serenity Prayer below:

   God,
   grant me the serenity to accept the things I cannot change,
   courage to change the things I can,
   and wisdom to know the difference,
   living one day at a time,

enjoying one moment at a time,
accepting hardship as a pathway to peace
taking as Jesus did, this sinful world as it is,
not as I would have it,
trusting that You will make all things right
as I surrender to Your will,
so that I may be reasonably happy in this life
and supremely happy with You forever in the next.

MY REFLECTIONS ON STEP TEN

Each day I do a review of myself and my activities. When I am wrong, I quickly admit it. When I am right, I thank God for the guidance.

1. Recall people and events in their sequence.
2. Ask God to forgive us.
3. Forgive others if they have hurt us.
4. Ask individuals to forgive us.
5. Thank God for the good things that have happened in and around and through us on this day.
6. Close the door to the day—forgive and forget.

For the person who is in Christ Jesus, there is no condemning, blaming, guilt, disapproval, sentencing, judgment. For the person who is in Christ Jesus, there is freedom (Rom. 8:1).

What do you think about Step Ten? Write down your feelings, thoughts, and ideas.

_____

_____

_____

_____

_____

_____

_____

_____

Exercise: Tonight, before you go to sleep, kneel beside or sit on your bed. Take six minutes to think through the day. Ask God to guide you in your thoughts. Be willing to do what He tells you.

For further study:

- Luke 12:1–3
- Romans 8:1
- Ephesians 4:25–26
- Philippians 2:1–4

CHAPTER 11

My Most Important Daily Appointment

<u>Step Eleven:</u>

To keep growing in my relationship with Jesus Christ, I spend time each day praying and reading the Bible. I will gather with others who do the same. I ask Jesus for guidance and the power to do what He wants me to do.

MY MOST IMPORTANT DAILY APPOINTMENT

Sitting in my office for about the tenth time was a very handsome twenty-nine-year-old man. All the young women in the area "noticed" him and talked about him. He was one of the most unusual young persons I had known. When he talked, his words had integrity. He had been raised in a healthy, loving family environment. Though his father was a driven financier, Joe seemed to survive with the minimal amount of time his dad gave him.

As we explored the areas of his life that he felt needed attention, we seldom found any problem or issue that Joe had not openly identified and was dealing with.

"I want more than anything else to live my life for Jesus Christ. He has loved me so much, the least I can do in response is to give Him my life," Joe said. When he talked like that, he didn't sound like a weirdo or Jesus freak. He was for real.

"I could spend the rest of my life looking at myself. I don't want that. I want to look at Jesus. I want to look at others. I want my life to count for something. I think the way it will count for something is to use my gifts in serving others," he said emphatically. He was sincere.

He wasn't denying his problems and issues. He simply wanted to put them in perspective and move ahead with his life.

"I don't want to get stuck on myself. I truly want to be a disciple of Christ. What does it mean to be a disciple in the late twentieth century?" he asked.

Joe, I thought, was a very mature person for his age. He had already outgrown the need to be "successful" or accumulate material things. His life was focused on all the right things.

Joe had gone through the Twelve-Step process many times in various forms. He had "worked" the Steps and grown immensely. He could relate very well to others and the kids he worked with in his church.

Because he had done so much work with the Steps, he did not live his life in compartments. He was the same person on Monday as he was on Sunday. His words, his feelings, and his attitude matched his behavior.

"It's what the Eleventh Step teaches that is making me feel so healthy," he said. "This Step is the single most important step I can do for myself. I spend the first hour of the day in prayer and reading the Bible. It has become the most important hour in my day."

Joe was at peace. He did not work at impressing. He was confident and yet knew his limitations. "I know I am young," he said, "but I think I am ready to keep moving toward the things that God wants me to do.

"And I study the Bible," he continued. "I carry a verse from the Bible with me every day. I read it often. I pray about it. When it's appropriate, I share that verse with one of my friends at work or socially.

"Each week, I get together with a small group of guys from my church. We talk about what's going on in our lives. We use these Steps to help us focus. And we pray for one another," he said. "I've been doing this ever since I was fifteen years old. I couldn't live without my brothers and sisters. I need their support."

Joe stands on a solid foundation. He is ready to do whatever God wants him to do. He is beyond "recovery" and into the great things that life has to offer.

Joe takes Step Eleven each day. He practices its four parts:

1. Keep a daily appointment with God.
2. Read the Bible.
3. Gather with others who pray and read the Bible.
4. Ask Jesus for power to do what He wants us to do.

Think about your life. How do you spend your time each day? This exercise will help you check it out.

Activity _____ Amount of time _____

Sleeping.._____

Eating.._____

Dressing/getting ready ...._____

Attending school ...._____

Participating in school activities ...._____

Talking on the phone..............................._____

Watching TV ...._____

Studying.._____

Reading.._____

Doing things with friends....................._____

Doing things with Mom........................._____

Doing things with Dad..........................._____

Having fun..._____

Going to church ...._____

Joining in church youth activities ...._____

Working..._____

Doing things with the family ...._____

Reading the Bible......................................_____

Praying..._____

Doing other things ...._____

_____

_____

_____

Total time _____

How would you like to spend your time? Who are the most important people in your life, and how much time would you like to spend with each one of them?

Person	Time
1. God	_____
2. _____	_____
3. _____	_____
4. _____	_____
5. _____	_____
6. _____	_____
7. _____	_____
8. _____	_____
9. _____	_____
10. _____	_____

If you could have a "perfect" day, what would it look like? Who would you be with? What would you do? Describe that day.

_____

_____

_____

_____

_____

_____

Now think about what a day would be like if you were living according to Step Eleven.

1. Keep a Daily Appointment with God.

The most significant thing you can do every day is to have an appointment with God.

Meeting with God is simple. He is available to meet us any time of the day. We do not need to make an appointment in advance. He has openings in His schedule all day and night long.

Meeting with God is important. He helps us choose what to do with our time and whom to spend time with. God wants to be very involved in our lives. And He is—when we let Him.

Meeting with God is a conversation. He listens and He talks. We listen and we talk. It is a two-way relationship.

Meeting with God helps us to see things from His viewpoint. God gives us an idea of what life looks like from a bigger picture than our small picture. Sometimes God lets us see how things look over the long haul.

Meeting with God is inspiring. He fills us up. He gives us hope and good reasons to live. God is the one who created life. When we meet with Him, He gives us new life.

Meeting with God changes us. We become more like Him. All of the great saints were shaped by their prayerful relationship with God.

Meeting with God is the best thing and the right thing to do. How do you feel about praying?

_____ I don't know how to do it.
_____ I haven't really tried it.
_____ I want to learn more about it.
_____ I am undecided about prayer.

Learn to take time for God. Try an experiment. Meet with God for six minutes each morning and each night. They will become the most important twelve minutes of your day. You will experience peace and guidance like you've never had before.

2. Read the Bible.

Another part of the Eleventh Step is reading the Bible. The Bible is a book of promises. It is a book that tells us who God is, who we are, and what God wants us to do. It is the best-selling book in the history of the world.

People who read the Bible on a daily basis find the strength, nourishment, and encouragement that they need. Each day they are given insights into their lives and the lives of others.

Most people who read the Bible have a reading plan. Each day they read a few verses and then pray those verses into their lives. They ask God for help in doing what those verses tell them.

Could you devote a few minutes of your day to reading the Bible? Check with your youth director or church. Either one probably has booklets to help you get started in reading the Bible. One of the best resources for daily reading of the Bible is Scripture Union, which offers publications for all ages. The number to call is 1-800-621-LAMP.

Another part of the Eleventh Step is about gathering with others who pray and read the Bible.

3. Gather with Others Who Pray and Read the Bible.

"Unless I get together with others who do this, I get messed up," one junior in high school said.

Sara, a senior, said, "The kids who do this—read the Bible and pray—are only a few kids in my school. I need these other kids because I start thinking I am weird. If I don't meet with them, I think I am all alone in doing this, and I don't want to be all alone."

"I need help in staying straight," Ted, a tenth grader, said. "So many kids in our school are into drinking, partying, and having sex. I know that none of that is right for me. But because so many others are doing it, they make it seem like that's all there is to do. It's not. Being with real friends who are into the Christian stuff is much better. I need to be with my brothers and sisters who believe this or else I will get eaten up by these others."

As we ask Jesus for guidance, He will give it to us. Many times He will give us that guidance through our parents. Sometimes He will give us guidance through these gatherings with friends.

The last part of the Eleventh Step is asking Jesus for the power to do what He wants us to do (not necessarily what *we* want to do).

4. Ask Jesus for the Power to Do What He Wants Us to Do.

Jesus promises to give us the power we need. He has the power to give. He gives it to those who are ready to receive it.

Jesus tells us to ask for the Holy Spirit (Luke 11:13) and wait until we receive the power from above (Acts 1:8). He tells us that He will send us another Advocate who will be our counselor, give us power, teach us, and remind us of what Jesus taught (John 14:16, 26).

He promises to pour out His Spirit on all humankind, that we will be filled with power and the Holy Spirit, and be given gifts to be His witnesses to the ends of the earth (Acts 2:4, 15–17).

When God calls us into a relationship with Himself, He does not leave us alone. He gives us power and guidance. He leads us moment by moment and day by day. He is with us.

TAKING STEP ELEVEN

Step Eleven reminds us that there are five important things we must do if we want to keep growing stronger.

1. Keep an intimate relationship with Jesus Christ.

2. Spend time each day praying. Make a list of people, events, and things that you will pray for every day or week. Begin this list now.

The people I want to pray for every day:

_____

_____

_____

_____

_____

_____

_____

_____

_____

_____

The events I want to pray about each day:

_____

_____

_____

_____

_____

Other things I want to pray for each day:

_____

_____

_____

_____

_____

_____

_____

3. Read the Bible every day. Try reading it first thing in the morning and last thing at night. Read the passages in this book. Get a modern translation of the Bible, like the New King James Version or Serenity, which is a companion for Twelve-Step recovery (published by Thomas Nelson, the same company that published the book in your hands).

When you read the Bible, ask yourself the following questions:
   • What is the point of this section of the Bible?
   • What insight into my life does this passage give me?
   • What do I learn about Jesus?
   • What action is God asking me to take through this reading?

4. Get together with peers who are also growing into these things.

5. Ask Jesus for guidance and the power to do what He wants you to do.

Begin taking Step Eleven right now by reading the following Bible passages about this Step and asking yourself the questions.

WHAT THE BIBLE SAYS ABOUT STEP ELEVEN

To keep growing in my relationship with Jesus Christ, I spend time each day praying and reading the Bible. I will gather with others who do the same. I ask Jesus for guidance and the power to do what He wants me to do.

Choose one or all of the passages from the selections given and read it or them each day during the next week. Think about the passage by writing your response to each section.

1. The Spirit led Jesus into the desert. There the devil tempted Him in three ways. After Jesus had gone through forty days of fasting, Satan tempted Him to make bread out of stones.

Jesus answered [Satan], "It is written: 'Man does not live on bread alone, but on every word that comes from the mouth of God'" (Matt. 4:4 NIV).

The point of this section is _____

_____

_____

_____

The passage gives me the following insight into my life:

_____

_____

_____

_____

I learn that Jesus _____

_____

_____

_____

God is asking me to _____

_____

_____

_____

2. Jesus told His disciples that prayer is a two-way conversation:

You may ask Me for anything in My name, and I will do it. If you love Me, you will obey what I command. And I will ask the Father, and He will give you another Counselor to be with you forever—the Spirit of truth. The world cannot accept Him, because it neither sees Him nor knows Him. But you know Him, for He lives with you and will be in you (John 14:14–17).

The point of this section is _____

_____

_____

_____

The passage gives me the following insight into my life:

_____

_____

_____

_____

I learn that Jesus _____

_____

_____

_____

God is asking me to _____

_____

_____

_____

3. Jesus also told His disciples to keep on praying, even if their prayers didn't seem to be answered.

Then Jesus told His disciples a parable to show them that they should always pray and not give up. He said, "In a certain

town there was a judge who neither feared God nor cared about people. And there was a widow in that town who kept coming to him with the plea, 'Grant me justice against my adversary.' For some time he refused. But finally he said to himself, 'Even though I don't fear God or care about people, yet because this widow keeps bothering me, I will see that she gets justice, so that she won't eventually wear me out with her coming!'" And the Lord said, "Listen to what the unjust judge says. And will not God bring about justice for His chosen ones, who cry out to Him day and night? Will He keep putting them off? I tell you, He will see that they get justice, and quickly. However, when the Son of Man comes, will He find faith on the earth?" (Luke 18:1–8).

The point of this section is _____

_____

_____

_____

The passage gives me the following insight into my life:

_____

_____

_____

_____

I learn that Jesus _____

_____

_____

_____

God is asking me to _____

_____

_____

_____

4. The apostle Paul told the Roman Christians that they didn't need to be prayer experts for God to listen to their prayers:

> **We do not know what to pray for, but the Spirit helps us in our weakness with groans that words cannot express. And we know that in all things God works for the good of those who love Him, who have been called according to His purpose** (Rom. 8:26, 28).

The point of this section is _____

_____

_____

_____

The passage gives me the following insight into my life:

_____

_____

_____

_____

I learn that Jesus _____

_____

_____

_____

God is asking me to _____

_____

_____

_____

5. Jesus Himself taught His disciples how to pray:

> **And when you pray, do not be like the hypocrites, for they love to pray standing in the synagogues and on the street corners to be seen by others. I tell you the truth, they have received their**

reward in full. But when you pray, go into your room, close the door, and pray to your Father, who is unseen. Then your Father, who sees what is done in secret, will reward you. And when you pray, do not keep on babbling like pagans, for they think they will be heard because of their many words. Do not be like them, for your Father knows what you need before you ask Him. This, then, is how you should pray: "Our Father in heaven, hallowed be Your name, Your kingdom come, Your will be done on earth as it is in heaven. Give us today our daily bread. Forgive us our debts, as we also have forgiven our debtors. And lead us not into temptation, but deliver us from the evil one." For if you forgive men when they sin against you, your heavenly Father will also forgive you (Matt. 6:5–14).

The point of this section is _____

_____

_____

_____

The passage gives me the following insight into my life:

_____

_____

_____

_____

I learn that Jesus _____

_____

_____

_____

God is asking me to _____

_____

_____

_____

6. Jesus spoke of the significance of group prayer:

Again I tell you that if two of you on earth agree about anything you ask for, it will be done for you by My Father in heaven. For where two or three come together in My name, there am I with them (Matt. 18:19–20).

The point of this section is _____

_____

_____

_____

The passage gives me the following insight into my life:

_____

_____

_____

_____

I learn that Jesus _____

_____

_____

_____

God is asking me to _____

_____

_____

_____

How do you feel about praying twelve minutes each day (six minutes in the morning and six minutes at night)?

_____

_____

_____

What is the next step that you could take to make your relationship with Jesus Christ stronger?

_____

_____

_____

MY REFLECTIONS ON STEP ELEVEN

To keep growing in my relationship with Jesus Christ, I spend time each day praying and reading the Bible. I will gather with others who do the same. I ask Jesus for guidance and the power to do what He wants me to do.

What do you think about Step Eleven? Write down your feelings, thoughts, and ideas.

_____

_____

_____

_____

_____

_____

_____

_____

_____

_____

Exercise: Today, I will pray at least twice: once in the morning, and once at night. I will ask God to help me pray more.

For further study:

• John 17

CHAPTER 12

Reaching Out to Others

Step Twelve:

I am grateful that God is changing me through these Twelve Steps. In response, I will reach out to share Christ's love by practicing these principles in all that I do.

REACHING OUT

Jim came consistently to a Twelve-Step group for several weeks. All of a sudden he dropped out. The leader called him at home to check with him and discovered that Jim had been in the hospital and was now recuperating from surgery in his home.

All the kids in the group sent him a card. Several went to visit him at his home. When it was time for Jim to return to school, two of the guys in the group offered to give him rides.

This is just one simple example of how kids can do the Twelfth Step.

I feel most alive and excited about life when I am sharing with others. When I am exercising my gifts for the benefit of others, I am energized.

The Twelfth Step is an action step. It challenges me to give as others have given to me. All of us have made it this far in life because others have given to us. It is our turn to give in response.

Before we push on to Step Twelve, let's review where we've come from because the review will encourage us. When we see where we have come from, we will realize how much good work we have done. We will see how ready we are to reach out and do the Twelfth Step.

A LOOK BACKWARD

You'll remember the First Step. In this Step, you admitted your powerlessness—you admitted your need for God's help.

In Step Two, you accepted the fact that you are in process...that your faith in Jesus Christ is growing and that He is at work changing your weaknesses into strengths.

In Step Three, you turned your will and life over to Jesus Christ.

In Step Four, you made great, and perhaps new, discoveries about yourself. You listed your gifts and abilities, maybe for the first time in your life. You started defining who you are.

In Step Five, you went (or you are planning to go) to God and another person to share with them who you are.

In Step Six, you got ready to receive Jesus' healing touch.

In Step Seven, you humbly asked Jesus to heal you.

In Step Eight, you listed those people you felt you needed to make amends with.

In Step Nine, you went to make amends (or you are still intending to go).

In Step Ten, you learned to do a daily review.

In Step Eleven, you learned to pray, read the Bible, and be with others who love Jesus Christ. You are also seeking God's power and guidance in your life.

These Eleven Steps have been preparation so that you can take this Twelfth Step. The Twelve Steps don't make us perfect. They do make us better and healthier. If you have done some work on each of these Steps, you are ready to do the twelfth.

Here is what one teen named Carol said when she thought of taking Step Twelve:

"I wish I had more time to spend helping the underprivileged, being with friends, volunteering to help others. When you're a teenager, you're constantly being stereotyped by adults, organizations, government, and friends. Everyone tells you what to do and be. I have a hard time just finding who I am now. We're not really confused, at least, not all the time. I have a definite plan for life and my future. Not all teenagers smoke, party, and rebel. I know of hundreds who volunteer, help others, and are probably more unselfish than many adults. Teenagers just have a bad reputation. Newspapers never discuss the good, always focusing on the bad. I see ten minutes during a newscast on a boy who murdered his parents but only two or less (or none) on the kid who goes every day to help the elderly. Basically, we want to be loved and respected, just like everyone else. Teenagers shouldn't be ignored. We're the next generation of adults, and we've got a lot to say."

By reaching out to others, the person doing Step Twelve gets the fulfillment that comes from helping someone else. The person who is being served gets needs met and feels cared for.

Twelfth-Step giving involves not only material things or time-consuming acts. It involves holding a door, saying an encouraging word, complimenting someone, writing a note, phoning a friend, shoveling a neighbor's walk, or volunteering to serve meals at a local charity.

There are kids who desperately need you. They are everywhere. Look around and see the pain and hurt. Kids need you to reach out to them, care for them, and love them. They need you to love them enough to tell them about what Jesus Christ is doing in your life. You don't have to be perfect. You only have to be you. Take the time to share your life with them—what you've learned. Invite them to your group (or begin a group with them).

Adults have the same needs. Your parents and other adults need you and your encouraging words as well. Reach out to the adults in your life. Do something to serve your parents. Tell them part of your story. Let them know what this process and Jesus Christ are doing in your life. Everyone needs to hear good news. You can bring that to others today. You don't have to wait until you are older or more educated or richer. You can do these simple things today, just as you are.

Jesus asked us to do this.

WHAT THE BIBLE SAYS ABOUT STEP TWELVE

I am grateful that God is changing me through these Twelve Steps. In response, I will reach out to share Christ's love by practicing these principles in all that I do.

Choose one passage from the selections given and read it each day during the next week. Think about the passage by checking the statements that describe how you feel. Then write a few words about how this passage applies to you.

1. Jesus makes it clear what He expects of those who want to follow Him:

> **If you want to be a follower of Mine, renounce yourself, take up your cross every day, and follow Me. For if you want to save your life, you will lose it, but if you lose your life for My sake,**

you will save it. What gain is it for you to have won the world
and to have lost or ruined your very self? (Luke 9:23–25).

___ Jesus, I want to be a follower of Yours, but do I have to take
up my cross?

___ Jesus, is there another way I could be a follower of Yours? Do I
have to renounce myself?

___ I want to be a follower of Yours, Lord Jesus. I want to lose my life
in serving You and others.

___ _____

___ _____

___ _____

2. This passage from the book of James was a direct challenge to
people who thought that they could coast into heaven. In James's day,
apparently some lazy folks didn't feel a need to give to or serve others.
James lays it on the line with them:

**My brothers and sisters, what good is it for someone to say, "I
have faith," if the actions do not prove it? Can that faith save
that person? Suppose there are brothers or sisters who need
clothes and don't have enough to eat. What good is there in
your saying to them, "God bless you; keep warm and eat well,"
if you don't give them the necessities of life? So it is with faith.
If it is alone and includes no actions, then it is dead** (James
2:14–20).

___ I confess that I have not been helpful to others.

___ I want my life to count for something. I want to put my faith
into action and give to others.

___ Please help me, Lord, to live out my faith.

___ Help me to serve others and give to them what I have to give.

___ _____

___ _____

___ _____

Others need you. Your family and friends need you. Other kids need
you. Many kids are so desperate that they are taking their own lives. You

can help. You can make the difference. Bring yourself. Bring your gifts. Bring Jesus to others. Let Him touch others through you.

In our training workshops I often tell the story of a man named Steve who lived in San Francisco and had decided to end his life. All the circumstances in his life led him to feeling hopeless. His mind was made up. He was going to take his own life. It was simply a matter of how he would end it.

Several days went by as he thought about the ways to commit suicide. The first option he thought about was to go to his office bathroom, cut his wrists, and die there. Concerned that it might be a messy affair, he thought about another option.

He would jump out of his forty-fifth-floor office window. That would be a quick way to end it all. On second thought, kind as he was, he remembered the possibility of landing on someone else and taking that person's life as well.

As he pondered some more, the best idea came to him. It would be best to jump off the bridge. Ah, that was it. That was simplest and cleanest. He put on his coat and mentally said good-bye to his office and belongings and quietly headed out to the elevator.

As the elevator was proceeding down to the first floor, he heard a voice say, "Give life just one more chance." Conscientious as he was, he was obedient and made a decision to do just that. *If the next person I see when I get off this elevator smiles at me and greets me, that will be my sure sign that life deserves another chance,* he said to himself.

Are you the next person that Steve will see?

Experience tells us that hundreds of "Steves" are out there. A simple smile and greeting could save their lives.

Step Twelve is about reaching out and giving yourself to others. You might have many "Steves" right in your school. Will you reach out to them?

TAKING STEP TWELVE

Check the items that you *personally* will do something about.

    ____ Write a note to Mom.
    ____ Write a note to Dad.
    ____ Offer to share my resources (computer, games, clothes).
    ____ Volunteer my time to help where I am needed.

____ Write letters to lonely relatives or others I know.

____ Tell my friends about Jesus Christ.

____ Write notes to my brother(s)/sister(s).

____ Call someone to let her know I'm thinking of her.

____ Invite a friend to this group.

____ Write a note to my teacher.

____ Help a friend with a project.

____ Write a letter to a missionary.

____ Give someone some of my clothes.

____ Give something valuable away.

____ Give money to my church.

____ Pray for everyone in this group every day.

____ Pray for one country in the world every day.

____ Give my friend a Bible for his next birthday.

____ _____

____ _____

____ _____

____ _____

Check the items that you think your Twelve-Step group (or youth group) might do.

____ Invite others to come to the group.

____ Begin a second group (break this one up).

____ Take a weekly collection. Give the money to _____.

____ Get each person in the group a Bible.

____ Support a mission.

   ____ Local

   ____ National

   ____ International

____ Go on a short trip together.

   ____ City (urban)

   ____ Mission

____ Work on a project to help others.

____ Visit shut-ins.

____ Adopt a grandparent.

____ Befriend a lonely or rejected kid in school.

____ Visit a hospital.

___ Pray for our school(s) and teachers.
___ Pray for all the kids in our classes.

___ _____

___ _____

___ _____

___ _____

___ _____

And there are other ways to fulfill the challenge of the Twelfth Step:

• Getting ready to do our life mission.
• Doing our best in school.
• Taking risks in exploring ways to make better use of our lives, gifts, and talents.

These we work at one day at a time, one moment at a time.

As Christians, our call is clear: to take the message of Jesus Christ to others all around the world. Missionaries have a call to serve others in a foreign land. We have our own outreach. It may be someone in our school or our church, our next-door neighbor, or a distant relative. We have the wonderful privilege of handing on the good news to others. Christ is here. Christ is alive. He loves us and accepts us just as we are. What more could anyone want?

My participation in small group meetings has given me unconditional acceptance, affirmation, support, encouragement, new vision, and renewed hope. As I meet with a group that uses this Twelve-Step framework, I am given the nourishment I need to go back out to my family, profession, and friendships. I am renewed and strengthened to love those I am with, even those who may sometimes be unlovable.

I have a great call and opportunity to live out the Twelfth Step. I am grateful for the challenge that it consistently lays before me. We all have a similar call. I praise God that He cares enough for us to give us this joyous assignment of loving and giving to others in the name of Jesus Christ.

1. I don't serve others more because

___ I don't know where the need is.
___ I don't know how to serve others.

___ I don't know how to begin. I want to serve, but I need help in getting started.

___ I don't have time for serving others. My hands are full already.

___ serving others is not my gift.

___ serving others is not a priority for me.

___ _____

___ _____

___ _____

2. To the best of my knowledge, here is my assessment of where I am with the Twelve Steps:

___ They have helped me a great deal.

___ I am now ready to serve others by reaching out to share the love of Christ with them.

___ I need another go-around with the Steps. Right now I feel inadequate to reach out.

___ I need more time. (That's okay; some people need years.)

___ I am working at putting these principles to work on a daily basis. They are working for me.

___ I am eager to share what I have learned with others. I am looking for a place to do that.

Sam Shoemaker passed on the principles of the Twelve Steps to Bill Wilson. And Bill Wilson passed them on through Alcoholics Anonymous to millions of other people whose lives have been changed forever.

Shoemaker wrote a poem, "I Stand by the Door," which explained the meaning of his life. Read this poem throughout the week as you think about taking Step Twelve.

I Stand by the Door*

I stand by the door.
I neither go too far in, nor stay too far out,
The door is the most important door in the world—
It is the door through which [people] walk when they find God.
There's no use my going way inside, and staying there,

---

*Helen Smith Shoemaker, *I Stand by the Door: The Life of Sam Shoemaker* (New York: Harper & Row, 1967), p. ix.

When so many are still outside and they, as much as I,
Crave to know where the door is.
And all that so many ever find
Is only the wall where a door ought to be.
They creep along the wall like blind [people],
With outstretched, groping hands.
Feeling for a door, knowing there must be a door,
Yet they never find it . . .
So I stand by the door.

The most tremendous thing in the world
Is for [people] to find that door—the door to God.
The most important thing any [person] can do
Is to take hold of one of those blind, groping hands,
And put it on the latch—the latch that only clicks
And opens to the [person's] own touch.
[People] die outside that door, as starving beggars die
On cold nights in cruel cities in the dead of winter—
Die for want of what is within their grasp.
They live, on the other side of it—live because they have not
    found it.
Nothing else matters compared to helping them find it,
And open it, and walk in, and find Him . . .
So I stand by the door.

MY REFLECTIONS ON STEP TWELVE

I am grateful that God is changing me through these Twelve Steps. In response, I will reach out to share Christ's love by practicing these principles in all that I do.

My Twelfth Step Prayer

Dear Lord Jesus,

There is so much to do. So many suffering people need me and my group. Give me the courage to reach out, to give myself to others. Help me to be more like You. Come into my heart, mind, body . . . all of me. Be my Lord. Help me to be Your servant so that I will serve Your people as You would want.

I love You, Lord Jesus. I want to love Your people as well. Please, day by day, show me how. Amen.

What do you think about Step Twelve? Write down your feelings, thoughts, and ideas.

_____

_____

_____

_____

_____

_____

_____

_____

_____

Exercise: Today, I will reach out to that one person who has been on my mind.

For further study:
• Matthew 5:13–16
• John 3:1–8
• Matthew 25:31–46
• Luke 15:1–10
• 2 Corinthians 5:17–21

The Twelve Steps to a New Day for Teenagers Group Leaders Resource Manual

Why The Twelve Steps to a New Day for Teenagers Was Written

I've put these materials together for many reasons. There are four dominant ones:

1. I have experienced frustration and "failure" in youth ministry. I often felt that we were only scratching the surface in our relationships and work with kids. I felt they needed more. I knew we had to do more to share with them about basic life skills. This Twelve-Step process does that.

2. Traditional youth ministry models have failed. "Pied Piperism" no longer works, if it ever did. Getting more adults to reach out to more kids is the only way youth work will expand as we look forward to the next century.

3. This approach works. I have done it and used it for years with all kinds of kids.

4. This material is highly adaptable. It is a platform for you to share your story with kids. This book provides a format for you and frees you to be with them, relating...rather than fretting about preparing for the next meeting. This tool is to help you do your work with kids.

This manual was originally prepared as an outline for persons participating in a group leaders' training workshop. Training sessions are available. You can write for more information at the address on page 212. Although developed for use with *The Twelve Steps to a New Day for Teenagers*, the information in this manual is valuable and transferable whenever the small group process is involved.

How and Where This Book Is Being Used

This material is being used in more than thirty U.S. states by the following groups and individuals:

- Youth ministry programs (some congregations are having the kids go through the Steps three times each year, with retreats in between twelve-week sessions)
- Confirmation classes
- Individual kids
- Personal discipleship
- Mentoring relationships
- Mission preparation groups
- Groups in schools (as an after- or preschool activity, fully acknowledging that it is a Christian activity needing the approval of school authorities and parents)
- Full-week summer camps
- Weekend camps
- Individual parents with a son/daughter
- Juvenile detention centers
- Parachurch organizations (Young Life; Student Venture)

How to Begin This Process

This manual is a tool, a resource, a starting point. Use it in the beginning and as you need it.

Pray about this. All through the process, rely on prayer.

1. Go to your pastor with these materials. Ask for his or her approval and help in establishing a group(s) or using these materials in an already established group.

2. Go to your youth minister/worker. Ask for approval and involvement in this process.

3. Work with the pastor and youth worker to develop a core of adults.

4. Develop a core of kids to start your group.

5. Talk about this idea with kids, one on one. Make announcements about it. Whet their appetites. Don't give them too much information at the beginning.

6. Announce an informational meeting. Personally invite kids to come. Tell them you'd like to try an experiment for twelve weeks. Are they open to it? Give them a copy of this book.

7. Begin with an overnight, a retreat, or a mini-retreat. Introduce the Steps and do parts of Step One.

8. Read through the manual. If you are anxious to get started and don't want to take the time to read the whole manual now, work through the "Walking Through a Meeting" pages. Use these pages as a guide for all meetings. Read the rest of the manual as you move through the Steps.

How to Use This Process

When you begin a group, think in terms of an ongoing group for at least one year. Take one step each week. After you have gone through the Twelve Steps and when you get to the thirteenth week, begin again with Step One.

As you are working your way through the Steps, select one or two interactive exercises from the step you are on, and use that as a way to help participants share.

Always break into small groups of four for part of the meeting.

Consider having several groups each week. (Afterschool, preschool, and evening options—the daytime groups usually feel more rushed. You need at least an hour and a half to get into things.)

Introduce kids to the groups through a sample talk (see sample talk in this manual) and through personal contact.

Introduce this process through one or two retreats. Focus on one or two steps at each retreat, and let kids get a feel for how well this process works.

Inform people in the community of ongoing groups for kids that are available at your church or neighborhood gathering place.

WALKING THROUGH A MEETING

Every group meeting is different. Each group approaches the meeting in its unique way. Some of the consistent elements in a group meeting are listed below. These are suggestions only. Please adapt them for use in your groups.

Here is a suggested agenda with time analysis:

- Welcome through Scripture reading: 10 minutes
- Small group sharing: 30 to 40 minutes
- Presentation/sharing: 10 to 15 minutes
- Closing and prayer: 10 to 15 minutes
- Suggested total meeting time: 90 minutes

Have a Group Agenda

The successful Twelve-Step group has an agenda that fits the group's situation. The weekly agenda given here is only an example.

Walk through one step each week for twelve weeks. On the thirteenth week, go back to Step One, and use one or two different exercises. The content of the book is not nearly so important as the sharing between the participants. Let the book be a tool to help you do your work with kids.

Before the group meeting

- What kind of group is it? Open or closed?
- Designate persons to be greeters at the door.
- Set up tables so that groups can gather around them.
- Ask leaders to come as early as possible to pray, share, and get set up.
- Set the tone for the meeting by playing some of their music as kids come in. (Be sure to turn it off during the meeting.)
- Begin and end promptly as you agreed to do.
- Have fun.
- Make each week's experience a little different from the previous week. Add a sense of adventure to each gathering. Lighten it up with humor when appropriate.

At the door

- Encourage leaders to greet the kids as they come in the door.

The meeting

- Ask one kid to read a welcome. *(See sample welcome below.)*

A Welcome

Welcome to this Twelve Steps for Teenagers group. We are here to support one another. What we share in this room will stay in this room.

Our group is gradually walking through the Twelve Steps, one step at a time. We are learning more about ourselves and how to live with our problems. We are together to help one another. We do this by sharing our feelings, thoughts, and ideas. We do not expect to be perfect. We are trying to become healthier.

You will find support here. During our sharing, no one person dominates the group. There are no memberships, no dues, no fees. You can remain anonymous. The group focus is on Jesus Christ and His willingness to help us in all of our struggles.

Please join us for at least six weeks before you make any decisions about whether this group can help you. We think it can and will help you.

Thanks for joining us!

- Introduce yourself and have the kids introduce themselves (first names only).
- Do a warm-up (everyone gets to speak at least once during the meeting). The following are some suggestions:
  - Depending on the group, you may sometimes need to do physical activity together.
  - Rate your day.
  - Describe your favorite room in your house and why it is your favorite.
  - What was the most fun thing you did today?
  - What do you do with your free time?
  - What are you most looking forward to right now?
  - Describe one good relationship you have right now.
  - "At this time last year, I was..."
  - "If I knew I wouldn't fail, I'd try..."
  - "One lesson I've learned the hard way is..."
  - "Some of the best advice I was given was..."
  - "One unfulfilled dream I have is..."
  - "You would know me better if you knew that I..."

- Take up a collection (optional). Proceeds can go to buy more books to give to others, to support missions, to buy Christmas gifts for needy families, or to meet other needs.
- Say the Serenity Prayer (see page 135).
- Read a statement of purpose. *(See sample below; it's to be read at intervals, or when the leader feels a need to call the group back to its basic purpose.)*

A Statement of Purpose

If we want to grow, we need to be honest. It is easy to lie to ourselves, but with the help of Jesus Christ, no cover-up is necessary. Through Him and His love and this group, we will receive the courage to make needed changes in our lives.

This is a support group. We are here to help one another. We will not criticize, condemn, belittle, or judge others in this group while with them here or outside this group.

We do not expect perfection of ourselves or others. We do expect to grow by being more honest with ourselves and others in this group. We learn more about ourselves by sharing. During our sharing, no one should dominate the group. Everyone has a right to share feelings. What is shared here stays here. Outside this meeting we can talk only about ourselves.

During the week, between meetings, we will try to be in touch with one another. Our goal is to grow up learning how to love Jesus Christ and one another as He told us to.

- Read the Twelve Steps for Teenagers—one step or all Steps. All read together.
- Read Scripture. Choose one passage or Bible story from each step as given in each chapter of the book.
- Present a step.

From their perspective, leaders appropriately share how this particular Step and the passage or passages relate to their lives. This sharing is about 5 to 15 minutes and is not a teaching but something from the heart. If possible, there should be two leaders per group.

The two leaders rotate in sharing. *(See notes below for help in preparing this presentation.)*

To help you and the kids lead a step presentation, use the following methods of preparation:

• Relax.

• Pray.

• Read the step and commentary for each designated chapter.

• Read the designated Scriptures.

> — What is the main point in this reading?
> — What insight does it give me into my life today?
> — How does this Step make me feel?
> — What do I learn about Jesus Christ from this reading?
> — What action is God asking me to take?
> — Where am I now with this Step?
> — What experiences have I had with this Step?
> — Where do I want to be with this Step?

• Share in small groups using questions from this book for each step.

> Choose one or several interactive exercises to get the group started in sharing feelings and experiences. (Remind the kids often that this is not a discussion group—it is a *sharing* group.)
>
> Four kids make up a group. (Be in the same group for six weeks? Mix girls and boys together?)
>
> Designate which person begins and leads in answering questions in the interactive exercises. (If possible, place an adult in each small group. If that's not possible, shorten the amount of time in small groups for the first few meetings, and designate which kid leads.) Monitor closely. Lengthen if you see the small groups are working well.
>
> Assign a specific "task"—identify the specific page number(s) and the exercises you want them to share about.
>
> Set aside a specific time for this sharing (30 to 40 minutes).
>
> Suggest prayer for one another during the small group time and throughout the week.
>
> Suggest contact with one another outside the group meeting.

• Return to large group gathering.

> Make announcements (very brief).

Share prayer requests and/or answered prayer.

Say a closing prayer (Serenity Prayer; the Lord's Prayer; open prayer).

A Way to Begin Groups

These points assume you have shared the materials with your pastor and/or leaders, and you have approval to begin a group.

1. Gather names.

    a) The names of people I think might be interested in coleading this group with me:

    _____   _____

    _____   _____

    _____   _____

    b) The names of people I might ask to join me as part of an adult core group:

    _____   _____

    _____   _____

    _____   _____

    _____   _____

    c) The names of kids who might be participants in the group:

    _____   _____

    _____   _____

    _____   _____

    _____   _____

    _____   _____

    _____   _____

2. Set the date, day, and time for the meeting.

_____

3. Determine the place of meeting.

_____

4. Arrange for the room. A small room is best; sit around a table if at all possible for the large group; make movable chairs available for the small groups.

5. Indicate your preference: to have an ___ open group ___ closed group.

A closed group has a defined membership. The same kids come most weeks. This type of group more quickly fosters intimacy but risks becoming "cliquish." After becoming quite familiar with one another, group members may not be as likely to let newcomers in.

An open group has changing membership. The number of people and the people in attendance can change from week to week. An open group is less intimate but is more capable of making newcomers a part of what the group is doing. Open groups are more likely to stay focused on their "task"—the Steps—and could be healthier in the long run.

My experience is that open groups ultimately are the most effective.

6. Set a date for your first core meeting. Obtain copies of books. (All kids need books that they can write in on a daily and weekly basis. It is usually best to order a supply to have on hand and distribute them to each person who comes to the meeting. We suggest that the book be a gift from the church or group, but if kids would like to buy a copy, they could do so.)

7. Begin publicity. _(See section in this manual.)_

There will probably always be a continued need for Alcoholics Anonymous, Al-Anon, Narc-Anon, Alateen, and others groups directed toward a specific addiction or compulsion. At the same time there is a great need for Christ-centered support groups that deal with all kinds of issues and help kids address compulsions, addictions, and phobias—not only those related to chemical addictions. The church is the ideal place for the development of these groups.

The most difficult part is to get kids to come initially. Once they come, they will get into it. The Twelve Steps will not appeal to all kids, but keep inviting them and others. The process of inviting kids is an important end in itself. The contact with kids, where you take initiative, is a very positive and important caring step for kids, even if they never show up at any of your meetings.

Realistically, the Twelve Steps for Teenagers group process is in many ways simply a reason to call kids together, have a platform where they can sit together, be real, share their issues, and be exposed to the love of Jesus Christ through the group and the Twelve-Step experiences.

The Twelve-Step small group process responds to the real needs and pain of kids and adults.

The Twelve Steps for Teenagers break the cycle, change the pattern, and confront dysfunctional life-styles:

- by supplying a gentle framework that models and invites sharing of real feelings.
- by inviting and encouraging talking.
- by fostering trust.
- by helping participants understand what is normal and abnormal behavior.
- by providing a safe, confidential environment.
- by giving participants true community (a much-needed extended family).
- by providing a clear focus on the person of Jesus Christ.
- by letting participants feel that their worth comes from who they are, not what they accomplish.

WHO WILL BENEFIT FROM THE TWELVE STEPS FOR TEENAGERS GROUPS?

The Leaders Benefit

Leaders discover for themselves a more centered life, a way to express their gifts, a group to belong to, spiritual growth, fun, revitalization, and a great sense of fulfillment. Leaders are involved in the most important ministry of the church. Without a concerted effort to reach kids, there will be no church.

The Teenagers Benefit

It is impossible to measure the value and impact of a Twelve-Step group for teens. However, here are just a few ways in which they will benefit from the group.

- They will be provided with a safe environment in which they can share. The group will provide nonjudgmental, true friends who will support them as they are.
- They will have encouragement to change, take risks, and grow. The group process will provide a "system" for wholeness and health, a gentle pattern for growth.
- They will receive a spiritual perspective—a new way to look at themselves freely and honestly.
- They will have an adult role model. You as leader will have gone a bit farther than them in their journey through life.

The Sponsoring Organization Benefits

The sponsoring organization will realize

- care for hurting kids.
- renewed focus on the basic and important dimensions of ministry.
- a place to refer kids.
- renewed members.
- growth.
- revitalization.
- the development of skilled leaders.
- much, much more.

KIDS' NEEDS

Reflect on your adolescent experience. You can easily identify with the numerous needs of kids. Check the needs listed that seem to be the most significant from your perspective.

____ Kids need to build their self-esteem.
____ Kids need more family life.
____ Kids need adult role models.
____ Kids need more encouragement and affirmation.

____ Kids need to belong to a small support group.

____ Kids need to be involved in helping others.

____ Kids need a relationship with at least one adult outside their homes.

____ Kids need to be loved.

____ Kids need more attention.

____ Kids need to belong to a church and be recognized as important persons in that church.

____ Kids need a place to explore who they are.

____ Kids need to be challenged.

____ Kids need to know the truth about themselves, their world, and God.

____ Kids need to be strengthened and encouraged to make positive choices.

____ Kids need to know themselves better.

____ Kids need guidelines about life.

____ Kids need better relationships with their peers.

Other needs of kids (from your perspective):

_____

_____

_____

_____

Suicide, alcoholism, sexual activity, drug addiction, and numerous other ways that kids act out continue to affirm their needs. These problems are only symptoms. In this book and in the following section you will read several direct quotes from kids about how they perceive their lives and problems. They need help in dealing with these problems, not just symptoms.

Working with kids is a matter of the heart, of getting to the core of life, of discovering and holding on to what really counts in life. The Twelve Steps for Teenagers address most of life's major struggles in a very positive manner.

The Kids' Perspective

Here are what some kids consider their biggest problems:

- "My biggest problem right now is trying to find myself and please others at the same time." *Jill*
- "My biggest problem right now is lack of confidence in myself. Sometimes I depend too heavily on other people to tell me who I am." *Jessica*
- "My biggest problem right now is that I'm in a fight with one of my best friends." *Julie*
- "My biggest problem right now is establishing myself in a new school." *Matt*
- "My biggest problem right now is learning how to feel good about the way I am. I'm way too self-conscious." *Beth*
- "My problem is getting my schedule to work out. I'm always very busy, and I need to find some time when I can just relax and not worry about all my obligations." *Art*
- "My biggest problem right now is my family life. It seems that we're always fighting. Every time I turn around they're telling me that I'm a brat or that I'm selfish, or they're telling me what to do. I'm also having problems with my friends. I seem to get sick of them." *Ellen*
- "My biggest problem right now is justifying my existence and trying to find my true purpose in life." *Brett*

WHERE DO YOU FIT IN?

This resource manual has been written to give you assistance in your outreach to kids. The manual, however, is only a supplementary tool. You are the primary resource. You have all that it takes to effectively care for kids.

As a professional youth worker, I have made the following assumptions:

1. Working with young people is not as difficult as we've made it out to be. This is relational work. The same principles of developing relationships with other adults are applicable in relationships with teenagers.

2. You, as a caring adult, can have a significant impact on the lives of one, several, or many teenagers. You can do this with kids. In fact, it is probably true that if you don't do something with kids, no one else will. And that is precisely why we have so many kids who are suffering today.

3. You, just as you are, human, with all of your personal hangups and foibles, are the greatest resource some kids may ever see.

4. You do not need a degree in youth work or theology. You do not need to wear special clothes, speak a special language (youthtalk), play a musical instrument, or be humorous. You, just as you are, caring for kids, letting God love them through you... that is the greatest resource for youth work.

Jesus' disciples were most likely not nearly as educated, refined, trained, cultured, clothed, and mobile as you are. Yet Jesus used those disciples and accomplished great things through them. He will do the same with and through you. He needs your willingness to be led. Every moment that you give to Him in this faith adventure will bring you fulfillment that you never dreamed possible.

5. Your experiences are invaluable. Of course, we all need fine-tuning, but you already know more than 90 percent of what needs to be known about working with kids. What worked with you as a young person—the basic stuff—will work with kids now. What turned you off as a kid will turn them off.

REFLECT ON YOUR EXPERIENCES
AS A TEENAGER

Would you have needed the Twelve Steps for Teenagers? Check the items that were true for you.

_____ Did you feel that you never had a break in life?

_____ Did you cover up your real feelings? Did you often pretend?

_____ Did you have many unanswered questions about God? About death?

_____ Did you sometimes do or say strange or shocking things just to get attention?

_____ Did you feel unloved, uncared for?

_____ Did you worry about your parents, brothers, and/or sisters?

____ Did you feel afraid?

____ Did you avoid going home because you disliked it there?

____ Did you consider running away from your problems by using drugs, alcohol, or other chemicals or by listening to TV or audio tapes?

____ Did you go to extremes to get people to like you?

____ Was it difficult for you to talk with your parents about important things?

____ Did you feel lonely?

____ Did you have trouble concentrating on your schoolwork?

____ Did you lose your temper often?

____ Did you have some things in your life that you would like to have changed and wanted to change for a long time?

____ Were there things in your life that you tried to change but couldn't?

____ Were you frustrated?

If you checked one or more, you would have benefited from the Twelve Steps for Teenagers group process.

THE SHAPE OF YOUTH WORK TODAY

In the past twenty years, the style of youth ministry has changed substantially. Many congregations now see the tremendous need for directed outreach to kids, and they are attempting to solve the problem by hiring a professional youth minister/worker.

That's good news because someone is now "on the point" for developing the youth work in general. That's bad news because some members of the congregation have absolved themselves from any responsibility for direct work with kids. "That is the youth worker's responsibility," they say. They have nothing more to do with kids.

Young Life, the largest and most effective interdenominational youth ministry outreach program in the world, reaches less than 6 percent of America's high-school kids. Most churches seldom get more than 10 percent of their kids' potential membership list to attend ongoing youth ministry functions. Many show up for recreational dimensions, but fewer show up for "religious training."

Adults must be concerned with and reach out to kids who are outside the walls of the church as well as those who are church members. *A professional youth worker simply cannot do it all.* Professionals are generally hired to guide adults and facilitate their ministries with kids.

More must be done. More must be done with more kids—NOW. We are in a crisis with our kids. The responsibility for working with kids belongs to all of us. The future of youth work is simply a numbers game. The more adults there are for kids, the more kids will be reached.

Through my involvement with kids in CCD (Confraternity for Christian Doctrine), Alateen, Young Life, the prison system, and other youth-related platforms, I have seen young people suffer immensely. Theirs is a quiet suffering that seldom gets expressed. Too often it culminates in self-inflicted death.

There is a great urgency to reach out to kids. We have the most wonderful privilege in the world—to let kids know that there is hope, that there is a reason to live, that God does love them. Luke 15 says that Jesus came for the sick and the lost. We can be an important extension of His ministry as He flows through and in us to the kids.

OUR CALL

Jesus made a tour through all the towns, teaching in their synagogues, proclaiming the good news of the kingdom, and curing all kinds of diseases and sickness. And when He saw the crowds, He felt sorry for them because they were harassed and dejected, like sheep without a shepherd. Then He said to His disciples, "The harvest is rich, but the laborers are few, so ask the Lord of the harvest to send laborers to His harvest" (Matt. 9:35–37).

Jesus made that tour to teach, proclaim, and cure. He has given this same "mission" to us. His compassion is as great now as it was when He was on His tour. Jesus cares about kids.

In many ways, many of today's kids are like the crowds described by Matthew. They are harassed by noise, temptation, distractions, materialism, and peers. They are constantly bombarded with "static" activity—sounds and challenges. Their spirits have little rest. They are in motion from morning till night (sometimes very late at night). They have no solitude. Kids must be given the opportunity, platforms, and models to learn how to cope with this harassment. They must learn how to have and make use of solitude.

Many kids are also dejected, bewildered, cast down, disheartened, depressed, weak, and troubled. In many ways, kids feel hopeless. They often have little guidance. TV has become their mentor and friend. They are truly like sheep without a shepherd, wandering about, seeking something to live for and die for, seeking something to believe in, hope for, trust in. They need to be challenged, encouraged, and nourished.

KIDS NEED YOU

Kids need sponsors, guarantors, advocates, adult friends, someone with whom they can have a one-to-one relationship. Kids need you. You have what it takes to care for them. You are the answer to someone's prayers. You are the laborer some kids have been praying for.

Kids need spiritual food and teaching. They need nourishment. They need the kingdom perspective. They are empty, bored, void, and bankrupt. You can give them what they need.

What we needed as teenagers, teenagers today need as well:

- A group, a place to belong
- A program for growth with all the right ingredients
- Friends
- An adult friend, model, mentor, guide
- Spiritual nourishment (If kids don't get this from the church, they look elsewhere for something that will feed their spirits.)
- Clean fun and adventure
- A good church family and recognition as valuable people in it

The Twelve Steps for Teenagers address these needs and more. You can use these Twelve Steps with kids who are detached from the church or anything spiritual as well as with kids who are seeking advanced discipleship.

You can do this! They need you to do this!

THE GOALS OF TWELVE STEPS FOR TEENAGERS GROUPS

The key words here are *integration* and *balance*. We seek health, wholeness, and blending of the physical, emotional, relational, and spiritual dimensions of life for kids. We want them to feel free to be human and to have a realistic view of the spiritual side of life as well.

Ultimately, the goals and accomplishments of your group will depend on you, the other adults involved in helping you lead, and the kids themselves. The material written in this book for the kids gives clear direction and guidance along the way; however, your affirmation and clarification of the written material will make all the difference in the world.

Generally, I believe the goal of this Twelve-Step process could be summarized in the following statement:

> We seek with kids to become wholesome disciples of Jesus Christ, fully equipped for life and service. We strive to accomplish this goal through the processes of community relationships, the Twelve Steps for Teenagers, prayer, and involvement with our own churches.

We recognize it is a process, and the Twelve Steps provide a gentle framework that allows kids to grow at their own pace and lets them be where they are at the moment.

HOW THE TWELVE STEPS CAN HELP TEENAGERS

The original Twelve Steps as well as many other Twelve-Step programs have been used for years and have helped millions of people. The Twelve Steps address all of life's major problems, issues, and struggles.

The original Twelve-Step program was and is still used by alcoholics. The Steps have been a simple, straightforward way for them to get the help they need to stop drinking. The Steps also help them to change those parts of their lives that made their disease worse.

For about thirty years, many other people have benefited from Twelve-Step programs by applying the Steps to their specific issues and needs. In groups like Alateen, the Steps have helped kids with alcoholic parents to cope with the horrible struggles that often take place in that type of family. Other groups like Narc-Anon, Al-Anon, Overeaters Anonymous, and Emotions Anonymous, to name a few, have also used Twelve-Step programs to improve the lives of their members.

The Twelve Steps for Teenagers are designed for all kids who need help with daily living. All honest kids know they can use all the help they can get just to make it in life. Besides the issues of daily life, every teenager has an unusual problem or struggle that makes life even more difficult. The Twelve Steps for Teenagers are helpful to kids any time but especially when hard times come along.

This Twelve-Step process is

- evangelization—contextual evangelization—exposing kids to the basics of the gospel within a context that they can understand. It begins with and works through their needs and where they are.
- discipleship—ultimate discipleship. Almost all the major concerns and issues come out of and are dealt with in this framework. Kids grow to become wholesome disciples for Jesus Christ.
- a platform for prevention. Kids learn from one another and the leaders what *not* to do.
- community in its truest form.
- "therapeutic"—not therapy. (Professional counselors are needed to help with problems that leaders are not equipped to handle.) These gatherings are therapeutic because they are safe places for kids to share real feelings.

GROUP COVENANT

Group leaders may want to develop a group covenant with some or all of the following components. This step is best done after the group has met three weeks or more. Many small group trainers consider the covenant to be a crucial part of small group outreach. These components are suggestions only. Please adapt them as you see fit.

The name of our group is

We will meet at *(beginning time)* until *(closing time)* each *(day).* The exceptions will be on _____

_____.

We will meet at least twelve weeks. After the twelve weeks, we promise to be honest in evaluating this group. We may very well keep this group going for as long as it is needed.

We promise to be honest to the best of our ability.
We will pray for one another.
We will do our best to come prepared.
We promise to help one another.
We will listen to one another without interrupting.

For this twelve-week period, we choose to be *(check one)*

____ an open group (anyone can come from week to week).
____ a closed group (a select group will come from week to week).

Date:_____   Signature: _____

(Please list and distribute first names and phone numbers of group participants.)

THE GROUP'S RESOURCES

The primary resources for the Twelve-Step group include the following:

1. The Scriptures (suggested for each step and for your own references). The primary text is the Scriptures. As much as possible, let them speak for themselves.

2. *The Twelve Steps to a New Day for Teenagers* book. This workbook has been created to get kids into themselves and into sharing with you and the others in your group. It is simply a guide, a means to an end. Use it as long as it works for you and your group.

3. You and your life experience. Important work and research have already been done for you in this book. Now add your personality and emphasis and life experience. Use the book and the group as a platform to do your tailor-made work with kids.

4. The group, its members, and their life experiences.

5. Jesus, the person.
    • Who is He?
    • What did He do?
    • Why did He do it?
    • What can it mean to me?

Other than these resources, few materials are needed. Primarily, you are seeking to relate to and build one another up in your relationship with Jesus Christ. Don't get snagged on the written material.

Reflect on your adolescence. What worked for you? What turned you off? Whenever you want to do what is most effective for kids, recall your experiences. Let those experiences help you in the way you approach kids.

Encourage the kids to write in their books and to do word studies in the designated Scripture passages. Encourage them to spend twelve minutes each day in prayer and reflection: six minutes in the morning, and six minutes at night.

The interactive exercises for each step are created to get the kids thinking. Ask kids to prepare for the next meeting by reading over the Step and the questions. Ask them to answer all the questions before the next meeting. If they come unprepared, as they most likely will, take a few minutes of quiet time at the beginning of the small group part of the meeting to let them finish their work.

Listen to the feelings behind the words they express. Pick up on where they are. Some kids will need a call from you after the meeting.

Help the kids interpret and apply the meaning of the passages. Emphasize and explain key words.

You may want to extend the time you devote to Step Four. Ask the kids to do their part by working on the Step several times during the week and month. Return to Step Four occasionally and ask them how they are doing with it.

THE GROUP PROCESS

Again, reflect on your first group sharing experience. Recall the anxiety and tension you felt. Being in touch with those feelings will keep you alert to the feelings kids may be having as they participate in their first meetings.

Kids need one another. They just don't know how to express that. Help them by verbalizing your experiences in this area. Be especially hospitable with newcomers.

Ideally, Twelve-Step groups for kids will include about twelve kids with two adults. If the group gets much larger than that, consider splitting off and beginning another group or breaking into two smaller groups for part of the meeting (each group led by an adult).

Most group members go through at least three phases:

1. Checking it out. Slowly revealing who I am, what I've been through, and what I'm dealing with now.
2. Feeling accepted. That includes feeling recognized for who I am, feeling valued by the group, and beginning to feel my own giftedness. (This can take months.)
3. Making progress. Members feel support to change, they contract to change, and they hold themselves and one another accountable for growth.

Groups generally have an enthusiastic beginning, go into slumps after several weeks of meetings, and eventually end up with a solid core with which you can work.

Early in the process, assess whether having a core group of kids as "officers" or group leaders will be beneficial. This idea has pros and cons. Each leader must decide after appraising the group's particular situation.

Occasionally do an inventory of the group. Ask yourself these questions: (1) Is the group staying on the Steps? (2) Are the adult group leaders sharing appropriately from their life experiences? (3) Is the group focusing on Jesus Christ? (4) Are kids sharing their personal lives and stories? (5) Are the Scriptures brought into each meeting? Are they shared? Are they brought to life? (6) Is the group sharing or holding back?

THE LEADER'S ROLE

Almost anyone can serve as leader of a Twelve-Step group. Most leaders have learned a great deal as they reflect on their life experiences.

Although they have much to offer, many leaders feel that they have little to give . . . or that their lives must be perfect before they can give leadership to a group.

"We minister best out of our weakness" is a familiar line. All the struggles of daily life make us, shape us, and mold us into the mature human beings that we become. The process and the impact of all those issues and struggles on our lives give us leadership abilities.

Leaders, while in process themselves, are also *emotionally and spiritually mature: examples* but not perfect; *alive with the love and divinity of Christ*, yet very human; *encouragers*, and sometimes needing encouragement; *in a trusting relationship with the Lord*, even in severe difficulties (2 Cor. 4:7–18).

Leaders are *willing to pray for and with the group and individuals.*

Leaders are *committed to the Scriptures*—not necessarily scholars, but they recognize, in faith, that the Scriptures are "inspired by God," the "Bread of life," "a lamp unto our feet." Good leaders let the Scriptures speak to them in their personal lives and in the group process.

The Scriptures are our primary resource (2 Tim. 3:16–17). This small group process is a way for all participants to get into the Scriptures and integrate them more thoroughly into their lives.

Leaders are *servants*. Leaders lead by being honest, open, and appropriately vulnerable.

Leaders *adapt* the material in this book to apply it in ways that are most meaningful to the people attending their group.

Leaders *encourage* and nourish others. They work on finding the best in others, drawing them and their gifts out.

Leaders *set the tone* of the meeting by being themselves and encouraging others to do the same through modeling.

Leaders *share themselves and Jesus Christ* with others in the group. They do this naturally. This sharing emerges from their struggles and relationships and flows out of the step for the week and the related feelings.

Leaders *facilitate* the meeting, keeping the meeting focused on one step, the designated readings, questions, and appropriate sharing.

Leaders *keep the meeting on track*. Recognizing that there are a variety of personalities in each group meeting, leaders know how and when to "intervene" to call the meeting back to sharing. They begin and end the meeting promptly as scheduled. They are attentive to the group process (respect silence). They share feelings and experiences. They share how the Steps and readings apply to their lives. They ask for help in logistical arrangements (coffee, sitters, collections, bookkeeping, book orders).

Leaders *work with other leaders.* Ideally, each group has two leaders...a male and a female. Leaders have an ongoing relationship with the pastor(s) or person designated to coordinate this ministry with them.

Leaders *have fun,* enjoy the process, and relax.

The formation and development of a Twelve Steps for Teenagers group ultimately depend upon God. Relax and trust. Enjoy the process. Let it flow: "Unless the LORD builds the house, its builders labor in vain" (Ps. 127:1 NIV).

Write out your greatest fears or concerns about beginning or developing a small group like this.

I am most afraid of _____

_____

_____

My greatest concerns are _____

_____

_____

Prayerfully turn them over to God; let them go, and trust that He will address these fears and concerns.

GOOD NEWS FOR GROUP LEADERS!

This is God's work and ministry. You are His vessel. The success or failure of the group does not depend on you, your skills, or your experiences.

Your strength, courage, and nourishment to convene and lead groups come from the Lord and your relationship with Him.

Please review these passages often. They will help you keep your leadership and ministry in perspective.

1. This is God's ministry. It began with Him. It belongs to Him, and it is sustained by God. As a leader, be faithful to your call. Leave evaluation to God. Let go of the results.

And for anyone who is in Christ, there is a new creation; the old creation has gone, and now the new one is here. It is all God's work (2 Cor. 5:17–18).

2. The greatest of all miracles is that Christ lives inside you. Your presence, as Christ is in you, is your greatest gift to others. Your "best ability is availability."

Let go. Trust in the Son of God. He loved you and gave Himself for you.

I have been crucified with Christ; and I myself no longer live, but Christ lives in me. And the real life I now have within this body is a result of my trusting in the Son of God, who loved me and gave Himself for me. (Gal. 2:20).

3. As a leader, you know the secret things of God. Mostly, you know that Christ is at work in and through you. Praise Him.

They are those to whom God has planned to give a vision for the wonder and splendor of His secret plan for the nations. And the secret is simply this: Christ in you! Yes, Christ in you bringing with Him the hope of all the glorious things to come (Col. 1:27).

4. You and all others seek fulfillment. What we seek we discover in Jesus Christ. He is our fulfillment. He is what we seek. As we discover this truth for ourselves, others in our groups will make the same discovery.

In His body lives the fullness of divinity, and in Him you, too, find your fulfillment, in the One who is the head of every sovereignty and power (Col. 2:9–10).

5. This verse presents our promise and hope. We need not do this or any ministry in our own strength. We can do it through Christ who strengthens us.

I can do all things through Christ who strengthens me. (Phil. 4:13).

TWELVE STEPS FOR TEENAGERS LEADER'S JOB DESCRIPTION

As a Twelve Steps for Teenagers group leader, I _____ (name) commit myself to the following minimums:

1. *I promise to pray for each participant in my group on a consistent basis.* This is the heart of outreach to kids. Let nothing take precedence over prayer. Devote time to it each day. Pray for the group. Pray for every individual in the group. Pray with others about the group. Recruit others to pray for you and the group.

Learn to seek and be at home with prayer and solitude. Be at peace with yourself and the quiet places in your life. Model this strength for kids.

Use the Serenity Prayer in your personal life and for all group meetings.

Pray about the Scriptures. For example, use the designated Scriptures for Steps One through Twelve in this book, and pray about the meaning and application of those passages in your life.

2. *I will prepare for the meetings.* Preparation begins with being in touch with yourself as a leader. Slow down. Relax. Let God work through you. Pray. Pray for each kid in your group. Pray about the meeting. Ask God to lead and guide.

The passages in this workbook will prepare you for the Step you will be on each week. Read them. Digest what they say. Make the story your story. If possible, identify with a person in the passage you've just read. See yourself involved in that person's life. Find the "good news" for yourself in the passage.

Give the story a name. Write out very concise, brief answers to the following questions:

• What is the main point of this passage for you?
• How does it make you feel?
• What do you learn about Jesus from it?
• What insights are you given into your life?
• What action is God asking you to take?

Now look at the Step that you are on.

• How does it relate to the passage you've just read?

• Is there something from your life that would be helpful to share?
• How do the Step and the passage apply to your life now?
• What could you appropriately share with the kids in your group?

Pray again, asking God to show you how to proceed. Always go back to the basics. Stick with the passage and the Steps. Everything will flow naturally from these two crucial dimensions.

3. *I will attend and participate in all the meetings* (one and a half hours per week). When I cannot, I will alert my coleader so that he or she can prepare and lead the meeting in my absence.

4. *I will attend a monthly meeting with other group leaders* (one to two hours). Develop a support group for adults. If possible, together or individually, enroll in the Twelve Steps for Teenagers training workshop.

Discover what helps you continue to grow most. Develop a plan for your personal growth, and follow through on it. This plan is essential for avoiding the usual burnout that accompanies outreach to kids. Think of yourself as a person who will be a leader on a long-term basis, not only for this year.

Your training process is continuous. It never comes to an end. We as adults need continuous spiritual nourishment, or we will have nothing to give the kids. Spiritual nourishment comes from a daily process of praying, meditating on the Scriptures and other readings, being with others who love Jesus Christ, and meeting with other adult leaders on a consistent basis.

5. *I will contact each person in the group outside the group meeting at least once every twelve weeks.* Keep in touch with the kids. Meet them outside the group meeting. Check in with them. Follow up on some of the things they share in the group.

Get feedback about how the group is meeting or failing to meet their needs. (But don't put too much emphasis on this.)

Help them individually, especially around Step Four. Be available for Step Five, or refer them to pastors and others for that Step.

Get to know their needs. Don't be a fixer, but let them know that you care and that you know where they might be able to get more help.

Occasionally suggest books or give a Scripture reading or article to them.

Do a group evaluation on the thirteenth week.

IDEAL CHARACTERISTICS OF THE TWELVE STEPS FOR TEENAGERS GROUP LEADERS

1. They are compassionate.

2. They are contemplative/prayerful. They devote time to prayer each day. They pray for the group. They pray for the individuals in it. They pray with others in the group. They solicit the prayers of others. They seek to learn and be at home with solitude. They are at peace with themselves and the quiet places in their lives.

The growing and primary work of group leaders is to pray and solicit the prayers of others.

3. They are "articulators of inner events" (Henri Nouwen, *Wounded Healer*).

4. They are risk takers.

5. They are enablers/facilitators of others and their ministries.

6. They are persistent.

7. They are visionaries.

8. They are biblically based (Ps. 1).

INFORMING OTHERS ABOUT YOUR MEETINGS

Personal invitation is the best way to get people to participate in meetings. Word of mouth always works best. Most kids need several invitations, but persistence pays off. Kids inviting kids is ideal.

Don't be discouraged by low attendance. Sometimes a meeting of two is very fulfilling. Sometimes it takes a year before the word gets out about your group and its importance.

To begin with, your personal calls to kids are the key. Consider your contact and invitation as important ends. If kids are willing to talk about themselves, use the opportunity to be with them in some of their struggles. Let your call about the meeting be an excuse to be in touch with them. Most kids are flattered to be invited to participate in a group like this. In their loneliness and isolation, your call means a great deal to them.

Write kids letters and then follow up with a phone call.

The following suggestions may also make your group known throughout your community and/or church:

- Use the Twelve-Step group as a way to reach out to kids in the neighborhood.
- List the group in your church bulletin. List which step you will discuss in the coming week.
- See if your group can be included in school announcements and the school newspaper.
- Place an article in the neighborhood newspaper.
- Personally contact clergy, police, and counselors to let them know your group is available to all kids.
- Urge kids to attend at least six times before making any definite decisions about whether the group is helpful to them.
- Have a supply of the book *The Twelve Steps to a New Day for Teenagers.* Use money from group collections to buy and give books to kids as they join the group.

Give a talk to promote your Twelve-Step group. Talk to kids in your church, at your youth group, at service clubs, in schools, and anywhere else you think kids might be available to hear about this idea. *(See the sample talk below.)*

Sample Talk

I am excited about something new. Something that kids are getting a lot out of. It's called the Twelve Steps for Teenagers.

It's for teenagers who want to take some life-changing steps to improve their lives. This group will meet every *(state the day of the week)* at *(time)* at *(location)*. It will end at *(time)*. The book we will be using is available at the group meeting.

This group is here because kids all over America have expressed the need for such a group. Kids want a safe place where they can talk about who they really are. They want to talk over their problems, ideas, and dreams in an atmosphere where people will accept them.

If you are interested in this group, call me at *(phone number)*, or talk to me at the end of this presentation. My name and number are also in the church bulletin today. If you are interested in the group but the day and time won't work for you, please call me. We'll be starting other groups.

This group follows a Twelve-Step format that identifies the person of Jesus Christ as the "higher power." We all need the presence, love, acceptance, and forgiveness of Jesus Christ. We all have an area of our lives that is unmanageable. We all need to be more together with ourselves, other people, and God.

This group is not a Bible study or counseling group. It is a support group, with kids helping one another by walking through the Twelve Steps for Teenagers. The group does not end with Step Twelve. This group will always be here for you.

Each group has at least one adult serving as a leader. These adults volunteer their time because they care about what kids are going through. There are no dues, fees, or memberships. Simply come as you are.

There must be kids and adults sitting in this gathering today who have a need for this kind of group. Please be willing to let me or others know of your interest. Please see me after this talk, call me later, or look at the material in the back of the room.

See you on *(meeting day)*!

A SCRIPTURAL MODEL FOR COMMUNITY, SMALL GROUPS, AND OUTREACH MINISTRY

They devoted themselves to the apostles' teaching and to the fellowship, to the breaking of bread and to prayer. Everyone was filled with awe, and many wonders and miraculous signs were done by the apostles. All the believers were together and had everything in common. Selling their possessions and goods, they gave to anyone as he had need. Every day they continued to meet together in the temple courts. They broke bread in their homes and ate together with glad and sincere hearts, praising God and enjoying the favor of all the people. And the Lord added to their number daily those who were being saved (Acts 2:42–47 NIV).

The early church was a model for community, small groups, and outreach ministry.

1. It was a learning church. Members learned

   • about Jesus Christ.
   • from their experiences about Him.
   • what He taught them.

2. It was a praying church. Prayers included

   • praise.
   • requests for direction (dependence upon Him).
   • intercession for brothers and sisters.

3. It was an alive church. Things were happening: prayer; teaching; signs and wonders.

4. It was a united church: one purpose; one mind; one in spirit (personal agendas were set aside).

5. It was a sharing church—they gave to anyone in need.

6. It was a worshiping church.

7. It was a growing church.

   • Growth was a by-product.
   • Outsiders were attracted.

This is a model for our time. This is what our people are crying out for. This is the work of the church:

To believe in the One that God has sent, Jesus Christ (John 6:29).

To love one another so that the world will know we are His disciples (John 13:34–35).

These are the objectives of Twelve Steps for Teenagers groups.

A VISION FOR AN INTEGRATED YOUTH MINISTRY

It is a ministry of the heart (Eph. 4:18), primarily these traits:
- Compassion
- Sharing
- Appropriate intimacy
- Meeting real needs

2. It is a ministry of prayer, individually and corporately, characterized by contemplation, helplessness, and healthy dependence.

3. It is a ministry led by lay adults.
- They are available.
- They seek their ministry.
- They can make long-term commitments.
- They can easily start and administer it.
- They are "wounded healers."
- Their needs include training, ongoing nourishment, a monthly support meeting, and prayer.

4. It is a ministry of small groups within a large group context.
- The suggested ratio is one to four.
- Members interact throughout the week and between meetings.

5. It is thoroughly scriptural.

6. It focuses on Jesus Christ; He is worshiped, loved, and served.

7. It thrives on congregational prayer.

8. It progresses continuously through the Twelve Steps for Teenagers.

CHARACTERISTICS OF THE TWELVE STEPS FOR TEENAGERS

1. Personal vs. programmatic
   - The Steps address personal needs.
   - Personal contact is significant.
   - Program is the framework/adapted.

2. Experiential vs. didactic/cerebral/theoretical
   - Immediate application/integration is possible.
   - How does this fit or work—not only theory—is explored.

3. Formation vs. Information
   - Character development, molding, process—more than teaching "data."

4. Scripturally based and centered
   - They permeate the day; ask different questions; bring clarity.

5. Process vs. curriculum completion

6. Integration vs. compartmentalization

7. Means to an end (an excuse)—not an end in itself

8. Jesus focused vs. self- or issue focused

9. Faith life (adventure) vs. "sight" life

10. Balance vs. intensity

11. Therapeutic (not therapy) and preventive

12. Sharing vs. discussion

A SUGGESTED TRAINING PROCESS FOR GROUP LEADERS

Check with your pastor for small group leader certification requirements.

There are two major dimensions to leadership training: (1) initial orientation/training and (2) ongoing training.

1. The initial orientation/training is a workshop for group leaders and is an important orientation to group process and the unique integration of the Steps with the Scriptures.

2. Ongoing training involves several elements.

All leaders need continuous nourishment and input. They need feedback, evaluation, affirmation, and direction. Meetings for leaders need to be held on a consistent (monthly?) basis.

Ideally, leaders are themselves in a Twelve-Step process where they are not required to give leadership. This is a support group for a leader.

Ideally, all leaders have a "sponsor." A sponsor has also been described as mentor, soul-friend, guarantor, discipler, encourager, spiritual director... a relationship that is bound together in mutual love, care, and concern. This relationship is important to avoid burnout and keep on the positive edge. It is also good for modeling to group members the concept of "sponsorship."

Hold a training workshop for new and potential leaders twice each year. (Many potential leaders are group participants.)

Provide workshops/seminars focusing on specific steps or themes. (Ron Keller and Associates is available to help leaders organize evening, morning, half-day, one-day, or two-day seminars or workshops. See page 212 for information on how to reach the ministry.)

SOME SUGGESTIONS—DO'S AND DON'TS

1. Concentrate on one Step at each meeting. Read the Step. Read and integrate the Scripture references.

Have a Step/Scripture presentation/sharing from a leader who is applying the Step and passages in his or her life.

Eventually pass presentations around and give kids an opportunity to share—the sooner participants share part of their story in small groups and with the whole group, the more committed they become— but be ready as the leader for the times when they do not come prepared to share something or when they share something that does not have enough substance.

2. Focus on Jesus Christ. Jesus is the center, not ourselves, our group, or our issues. Be sure the group integrates His person and relevant characteristics (love, forgiveness, acceptance, presence).

3. Be prepared to recommend professional help for kids who have issues deeper than your support group can handle. Usually, your intuition will let you know when this recommendation is right.

Know other referral resources (pastor, pastoral care people, counselors). It is best if you know these people and their counseling framework. These counselors *must* be supportive of the Christ-centered perspective. Be confident that they will supplement the good work going on in the group. Ask for your pastor's help in this area.

4. Relax.

5. Listen.

6. Don't push, teach (this is not a class, but a process), give advice, or "parent."

7. Don't "control" the meeting. Let it flow. You are in a facilitative role. Start and end the meeting. Let the Holy Spirit prompt participation and control the meeting. Step back and let the meeting happen.

8. Don't be the focal point of the meeting. (Group members should not look to you for approval or comment after sharing.)

9. If at all possible, bring Bibles to the meetings. Get a supply that are all the same translation. When making reference to scriptural passages, refer to page numbers. Don't assume that kids know how to navigate in the Scriptures. (In fact, never assume anything about them.) Help them to avoid embarrassment.

10. Don't put anyone on the spot to read. Read as a group, or if you prefer to have individuals read, please ask them if they would like to do so, fully acknowledging that some kids don't like to read aloud.

11. Never put anyone on the spot to share. Always give the freedom to pass. (Some participants have come for months without saying anything.)

12. Be aware that this is not a support group for the leader.

13. Recognize that an ideal group size is about ten to twelve participants. An ideal small group size is four participants, with one person as facilitator. An occasional meeting of all groups and leaders from several congregations or the community will provide a format for celebration and encouragement.

14. Ask leaders to commit to leading a group for at least one year. That period of time is essential for the group to become established and known throughout the community.

15. Anticipate the main obstacle to involvement in this process. "Why do I need this kind of group if I am not in a crisis or chemically dependent?" Most people need this life-style.

16. Provide each teen with a book. The book is a tool to help kids write their own life story. Urge them to write, draw, or doodle. At the beginning of the process don't be surprised by the little preparation they do. Give them time at each meeting to review or prepare responses to questions.

17. The first time kids walk through these Steps, anticipate an exploratory attitude and a more intellectual approach. Only after going through the Steps the first time will they have an overview of the process

and begin to grasp the importance of actually "working the Steps." Don't expect too much. This life-style is subtly caught.

18. Anticipate fluctuating attendance. Don't assume it is a reflection on you or your leadership.

19. Think of this group process as an excuse to build long-term friendships. One of the main purposes of this process is to build real and lasting relationships.

20. Don't be anxious about finishing the book, lesson, questions, or section. The book has a great deal of material. It is to be used many times. Tailor each meeting according to the needs of participants. Let the book be your tool to begin the process. The objective is to help one another discover Jesus Christ and the depth in His Word. Get into the Scriptures and concentrate on them as quickly as possible.

21. Keep in mind that Twelve-Step process is really a healthy platform for

- preventive sharing.
- contextual, wholesome evangelization (the simple basics of the faith presented in a way that meets real, identified needs).
- concentrating on Jesus Christ the person.
- seeing how the issues and circumstances in our lives can draw us into a closer relationship with God and others.
- bringing perspective to our lives (putting issues, worries, and concerns into their proper place).

22. Create a climate of acceptance. Teach kids to tolerate one another. Don't let them put one another down. Teach them to affirm one another, their feelings, and their expressions.

23. Encourage kids to share their feelings. It is not a discussion group where people share only their ideas. It is a sharing group where people share their real feelings and expose who they really are.

24. Sit in a circle around a table (or several tables pushed together).

WHAT MAKES THE TWELVE STEPS FOR TEENAGERS DISTINCTIVE?

For years, Christians have sought the renewal and depth that came from Alcoholics Anonymous communities. They wanted the benefits of Alcoholics Anonymous, along with clearly identifying Jesus Christ as the higher power. This identification does not negate the long-standing, life-changing work of Alcoholics Anonymous or other groups that have broader appeal or concern with first-stage recovery. It is simply a matter of calling our Savior by His name, not to be divisive, but to be clear and specific for our own sake and for the sake of others who are sincerely seeking Christ.

We humbly use the name of Jesus Christ as He instructed us to do. Our group is founded on Him. He is the Foundation, the Way, the Light, the Bread of Life, the Truth. Life is rich and full because of Him and His presence in our lives. We celebrate His love and good works among us. We rejoice that we can say His name. He is our Savior... not our group, our "program," the Twelve Steps, or ourselves. He is the power beyond and higher than ourselves.

To Him, we admit our helplessness. We acknowledge Him as Lord. Our motive for calling on Jesus is not to be controversial, but to provide others and ourselves the opportunity to openly share the "name above names."

For further study, see the book of Colossians; Philippians 2; and John 10–17.

KNOW AND REVIEW THE TWELVE ASSUMPTIONS ABOUT OURSELVES

Read them at least monthly at group meetings.

1. Everyone can benefit from being involved in this group.

2. Everyone in this group is created in the image of God and has not yet discovered all of the good that is within.

3. We will find our potential and fulfillment in the person of Jesus Christ and groups like this.

4. The more I risk in this group, the more I will grow.

5. The group will help me as I become more willing to change; however, I am ultimately responsible for making the choices for myself.

6. The Holy Spirit has given every person in this group gifts to share with one another.

7. Scripture is our guide for life.

8. In order to become whole and healthy, I have to be attentive to my body, mind, and spirit.

9. I will celebrate who I am because of what Jesus and this group have done for me.

10. I discover more of who I am by sharing myself with you.

11. I want to be known as I am, even though I am afraid of that. I also want to know other kids as they are.

12. Jesus Christ has come to set me free and to bring me a full life. This group process helps me to see Jesus and myself more clearly so that I can become freer and have the full life as it has been promised to me by Jesus.

THE TWELVE TRADITIONS FOR LIFE IN CHRIST

Read them monthly at meetings.

1. Jesus Christ is our identified higher power: "Jesus Christ is the visible expression of an invisible God" (Col. 1:15). Our spiritual growth depends on faith in God and trust in Jesus Christ.

2. All men and women are in need of the presence, love, acceptance, and forgiveness of Jesus Christ. All are human. All have sinned.

3. In our group, there is only one ultimate authority, a loving God. God works through our group conscience and our group leaders. Our leaders are servants. They do not control or govern the meeting or group.

4. The Twelve Steps have universal application. Everyone has unmanageable parts of life. The only requirement for participation in our group is a desire to grow.

5. Our group's purpose is to encourage one another as we struggle with life's issues and draw one another closer to Jesus Christ, the source of life.

6. Each group is self-supporting and does not accept contributions from any outside source.

7. Confidentiality is the foundation on which our group stands. What is shared in our meetings stays in our meetings.

8. Everyone attending a group meeting has the option to speak or be silent.

9. Prayer is an important part of our meetings, but everyone attending has the option to pray silently, aloud, or not at all.

10. There are no right or wrong answers in the group. Our group will not give advice or judge one another. We are committed to supporting one another. (There may be a need and time for confrontation but only as Jesus prescribed it be done in Matthew 18:15–18.)

11. Our common purpose is to grow in the likeness of Jesus Christ. Our bond and our unity will come from our focus on Christ and our love for one another.

12. The Twelve Steps are positive and hopeful. They acknowledge that we are in the process of becoming . . . moving toward the fulfillment that we seek.

YOUR CALL TO LEADERSHIP

Group leaders are needed to convene and facilitate meetings.

You can do this. You are needed to lead a group.

Our world is filled with kids who are in great pain. You can be the one who begins a process of renewal, revitalization, and healing. Thousands, perhaps millions, have given praise for what Jesus Christ has done for them through small groups, the community, the Twelve-Step process.

You are on the verge of a great adventure.

You already have most of the skills you need.

You already know most of what you need to know—your life experience has taught you that.

You are the greatest resource your group will ever have.

You have the ability to adapt resources to the specific needs of the people in your group.

This is your call to leadership. You can do this. You must do this. Others are dependent upon you to begin and continue this process.

This is an exercise in faith. If you don't feel ready, GOOD. No one is ever ready, qualified, or trained for it. It is a joyous adventure that is rewarding for both the kids and the adult leaders.

OUR MANDATE

What we have heard and known for ourselves, and what our ancestors have told us, must not be withheld from their descendants but must be handed on by us to the next generation.

What must be handed on is: the titles of the Lord, His power, and the miracles He has done.

When He issued the decrees for Jacob and instituted a Law in Israel, He gave our ancestors strict orders to teach it to their children; the next generation was to learn it, the children still to be born.

And those in their turn were to tell their own children so that they, too, would put their confidence in God, never forgetting God's achievements, and always keeping His commandments (Ps. 78:1–7).

We must give the next generation what we have been given. As you reread the passage from the psalm, underline the specific things that speak to you.

Psalm 78:1–7 is a clear mandate. Our young people deserve to hear what the psalmist has ordered. The truth must not be withheld from kids. Kids must know the *titles of the Lord.* Kids deserve to know God's names and the implications of those names. God has titles from the Old and the New Testaments. Here are the titles given to Jesus: Prince of Peace, Mighty God, Wonderful Counselor, Holy One, Lamb of God, Prince of Life, Lord God Almighty, Lion of the Tribe of Judah, Root of David, Word of Life, Author and Finisher of Our Faith, Advocate, The Way, Dayspring, Lord of All, I Am, Son of God, Shepherd and Bishop of Souls, Messiah, The Truth, Savior, Chief Cornerstone, King of Kings, Righteous Judge, Light of the World, Head of the Church, Morning Star,

Sun of Righteousness, Lord Jesus Christ, Chief Shepherd, Resurrection and Life, Horn of Salvation, Governor, The Alpha and Omega.

Kids need exposure to the *power of God*—the biblical teachings on God's power as well as contemporary experiences with His power. God's response to the prayers of a Twelve-Step group can have a lifelong impact on a kid's heart.

Kids also need to know about the *miracles God* has done, in biblical times and in their own lives.

TWENTY-NINE WAYS TO HELP YOUR TWELVE-STEP GROUP GROW

1. Be sure to work the Twelve Steps. Stay on them.

2. Focus clearly on Jesus Christ.

3. Be sure to read and share about the Scripture references for each of the Twelve Steps.

4. Gather a core group to pray about your group.

5. Call others to pray about your group.

6. Have each person in the group call one other person to invite them to come to the group.

7. Publish the Step you are on for the week in your church bulletin. Invite others to come.

8. Hang group information on the church bulletin board and neighborhood community billboards.

9. Give a talk at your church.

10. Call an individual whom you know could benefit from the group. Invite that person to come. The best invitations are personal. Give that person a ride to the meeting.

11. Write a "blurb" for your church bulletin citing how the group has helped you or some kids in your group.

12. Go to Twelve Steps for Kids leader's training.

13. Send someone from your church or community to Twelve Steps for Kids leader's training.

14. Pray for each person in your group.

15. Go to the Stephen's Ministry coordinator in your congregation. Ask him/her to make referrals to your group.

16. Distribute business cards with your group name, times, and phone numbers.

17. Call the neighborhood newspaper.

18. Write notes to those who come and to those who came.

19. Don't be overly concerned with the size of your group.

20. Use music (at the beginning of the meeting).

21. Do a Twelve-Step retreat at your church.

22. Have a one-night focus on one of the Steps (3 hours).

23. Pray for those who could benefit from your group. Ask the Lord how you could serve them.

24. Don't get discouraged (1 Cor. 15:58).

25. Take a risk. Share more of your real self with your group (model openness).

26. Meet kids one by one. Go to them.

27. Establish a prayer chain. Begin the chain with a request for prayer for something personal.

28. Tell your pastor what you need from him/her.

29. Pray about all of these ideas. Does the Lord want you to use any of them in your group?

*For more information on
training workshops,
retreats,
or a brochure on our
services,
please write:*

Ron Keller and Associates

6104 Russell Avenue South
Minneapolis, Minnesota 55410
or call 612-920-8428

What Does the Writer Know About the Twelve Steps for Teenagers?

Ron Keller has done extensive work with the Twelve-Step process through Alateen, Adult Children of Alcoholics, Al-Anon, small groups, and Twelve Steps for Christian Living groups. As program director for the Institute for Christian Living, he developed and implemented a training program for group leaders.

He was an area/regional director of Young Life for thirteen years. He served on the North Dakota State Pardon Board for eleven years, and on the Heartview Alcoholism Treatment Center Board for seven years. Mr. Keller is the former chair of the department of youth ministry at Barrington College in Barrington, Rhode Island. He has been a consultant/trainer for Youth Forum, Youth Leadership, Tentmakers, the Catholic Church, Renew, and the Institute for Christian Living. He is an adjunct professor at Luther/Northwestern and Bethel Seminaries in Minneapolis and St. Paul and has an M.A. in theology from Fuller Seminary.

He helps churches and schools develop small groups, and he does spiritual counseling for individuals and couples.

He is also a sailor and a writer. He and his wife, Nancy, live in Minneapolis, Minnesota, and have five children, four of whom are teenagers.